SPEAKING
OUT:
AN
Introduction
TO
Public Speaking

A student-friendly guide to public speaking

MICHAEL GALLAGHER

MERIWETHER PUBLISHING
A division of Pioneer Drama Service, Inc.
Denver, Colorado

Meriwether Publishing
A division of Pioneer Drama Service, Inc.
PO Box 4267
Englewood, CO 80155

www.pioneerdrama.com

Editor: Theodore O. Zapel
Assistant editor: Amy Hammelev
Cover design: Jan Melvin

Library of Congress Cataloging-in-Publication Data

Gallagher, Michael.
    Speaking out : an introduction to public speaking : a student-friendly guide to public speaking / Michael Gallagher. -- 1st ed.
        p. cm.
    Includes bibliographical references.
    ISBN 978-1-56608-161-0
  1. Public speaking--Juvenile literature.   I. Title.
    PN4129.15.G35 2010
    808.5'1--dc22

                                                                  2010037529

2   3   4   17   18   19

For Evşen

Contents

Introduction

"Speak the speech I pray you."
— Shakespeare (*Hamlet* III, ii, 1)

As a student of public speaking you may ask yourself the question: "What can public speaking possibly do for me?" My response is that ever since I began teaching speech years ago, when I tell people what I do for a living, they say one of two things to me. Either they say, "You know, I wish I would have taken the opportunity to work on that when I was in school, because I use those skills everyday and I know with practice, I would be better" or, "I sure am glad I took that class in high school because I use those skills daily and feel better for having had the training." I am convinced that students who practice public speaking in high school are preparing themselves for success later in life.

Think of all the times you need to use your skills in communicating. Whether it is to discuss a grade with a teacher or to borrow the car for the dance, the same skill set applies. As you get older, the skill set remains the same, but the stakes get higher. Instead of discussing a grade or a paper with a teacher, you may be convincing your boss to give you a needed raise. Borrowing the car requires some diplomacy, but negotiating the price of a vehicle is a life skill.

The practical skill set in public speaking is not just recognizing what you want, but providing you with a strategy for getting it.

Why Bother?

As a student, it is important for you to learn that public speaking is a life skill that you will use to improve you career, relationships, and understanding of the world. When the student editor of the school newspaper asked me the purpose of the speech and debate program, my response was, "To prepare students to be responsible leaders in the adult world." From personal experience as a high school student, the students who competed with me on my speech and debate team have gone on to become special individuals. Whether or not their speech activity had an influence in what they would become in the years following is a bona fide question. Yet the

1

fact that many of them went on to distinguished careers and they all had expert training in the world of speech and debate is more than just a coincidence. One student, after attaining his law degree at Cornell University and master's at Stanford, went on to assist South American countries in restructuring their debt. Another student runs his own headhunting operation in the Denver Metro area. His former debate partner worked as a diplomat for the U.S. Department of State. A state champion extemporaneous speaker now owns a power company in the Northeast. Another former debater is a partner in a law firm in Denver. The one thing these individuals all have in common is that they participated on not only the same speech and debate team, but also graduated from high school in the same year.

In the Denver area alone, business leaders, congressional representatives, and an anchorwoman participated in the world of speech and debate. Is this too just a coincidence? Notables like former presidents Ford, Johnson, and Nixon, and actors Tom Cruise and Shelley Long all participated in competitive speaking. Former presidential candidate John Kerry participated in the Yale debate program. Communicator of the twentieth century Ted Turner competed in his high school debate program. Could this all be just a coincidence?

Throughout the book are illustrations of the necessity of a public speaking background for personal and professional growth. Not only do those who perform at the upper echelons of society need the fundamentals of public speaking, but people from all socio-economic classes benefit from a basic instruction of public speaking. This book will show you how public speaking transcends the speech class to assist in every area of academic study. In other words, the skills learned in the public speaking class benefit you in your other classes. From explaining the complexities of the chemistry lab in science to demonstrating the importance of a historic event in history, the common thread is the ability to successfully present your ideas. Since public speaking provides an ideal platform to learn how to work with others, this book will also focus on the necessity of individual and group development using basic class activities. The idea that we can learn to work together in groups is essential to the overall importance of public speaking in society. Some would argue that to work on your ability to speak well is not only a personal benefit, but also an individual's obligation to help better society. So, by learning how to speak, you are putting yourself in a position to help your community!

One critical aspect to public speaking is listening. As a student in any class, success depends on your ability to gain the required information. A 1997 survey conducted by M.S. Peterson came up with the following conclusion: "Students with ineffective listening skills fail to absorb much of the material to which they are exposed. Students who are unable to effectively ask for help from a teacher, will not receive it, and typically reticent students progress more slowly despite what may be a normal level of aptitude" (Morreale, et al. 2). The emphasis here is that even though a student may select a background that has no apparent connection to public speaking, being able to articulate and understand pertinent information is crucial to his or her success. You will learn more about gathering information in Chapter Six: Listening.

Did you know that academic success can translate into career success? Even careers with little or no apparent public communication skills identify effective expression as a necessary skill. A survey sent to personnel interviewers at 500 corporations asked the question of what skills are necessary to enter into the business world. Of the 253 respondents, over 90% replied that, although communication skills are essential for success, many applicants lack effective skills in job interviews (Morreale, et al. 10). It only makes sense that students should have the opportunity to practice interview techniques before they apply for a job. Knowledge of basic public speaking can assist you in the very important life skill of anticipating and researching interview questions. Another report by the Business Education Forum, an organization of Fortune 500 executives, finds that although students have "highly impressive academic skills, graduates lack communication skills and the ability to work in teams and with people from diverse backgrounds" (Morreale, et al. 16). In other words, students leave colleges and universities without the basic training of being able to communicate.

One practice of basic public speaking should be to allow you the experience and practice of having to communicate in unfamiliar situations. This practice gives you some applicable training to react and overcome the challenges of new and different surroundings.

3

Say, for example, you want to become an accountant one day. The Accounting Education Exchange Commission stresses that all accountants should be taught basic communication skills (Morreale, et al. 21). In other words, how can an accountant achieve success without the ability to communicate what the client needs to know?

In concert with much of the importance of effective communication are the psychological aspects of achieving self-actualization. The same text describes the process of achieving this goal as "involving communication activities such as making contributions in groups, exerting influence over others, and using socially acceptable behavior" (Morreale, et al. 3). With so much of a person's cognitive and professional development riding on the ability to communicate, the conclusion is that you will benefit from a public speaking course. Providing a fundamental background in public speaking and communications also develops those skills essential to one's ability to contribute to the progress of a group project. The ability to combine socially accepted behavior with the skill of articulation necessary to influence others should improve society as a whole. Therefore, a primary goal of learning public speaking is to help the individual's psychological development, resulting in a collective benefit realized by society. Being trained in public speaking leads to positive social behavior. Did you know that the lack of effective communication can lead to delinquent behavior? For example, one study done by R.D. Clark and Shields points out that 339 high school students and parents were administered the Parent-Adolescent Communication Scale, measuring the extent of freedom of discussion between parents and children. The study's findings suggest that lack of communication is related to delinquent behavior and that good family communication deters inappropriate behavior (Morreale, et al. 11, 23).

Is it possible that public speaking is one of the greatest fears of most adults? My goal is to make sure you develop the confidence necessary to overcome any fear associated with public speaking. This piece of information adds to the challenge of taking a public speaking course. It is important for students to develop confidence to state their opinions, goals, and objectives. The primary purpose of this book is to help you rise to the challenges of public speaking.

It is important for you to realize that training in communication is an obligation of an individual to society. In 1978, Congress officially added "effective oral communication" to the basic skills of reading, writing, and mathematics for all schools (Public Law 95-561). Therefore, it is legally required for you to learn how to communicate. The reason for the establishment of such a law is that the art of practicing communication is essential to the progress of society as a whole. As a productive member of society, it is your duty to become trained in public speaking. Whether you want to continue to participate in the world of speech and debate or to simply be able to pursue a career with confidence, effective communication is not only necessary, it should be compulsory.

The logical conclusions dictate that while participation in the world of speech and debate may not guarantee world-renowned status, being in a public speaking program provides a background promoting prominence. When asked the question "why bother?" it is important to consider the overwhelming evidence that suggests life after participating in speech and debate can be fruitful.

Section One:
GETTING STARTED

Chapter One:
The First Day and Breaking the Ice

As a student, it is important that you are prepared for the first day. In addition to all necessary materials in your school "tool box," the most important tool at your disposal is a positive attitude. A positive attitude is perhaps the only thing we can control one hundred percent of the time. One strategy to help you maintain a positive attitude might be to think to yourself, "I can do this, I will do this, and I will try to have fun doing this." With a positive attitude, the chances of overcoming an obstacle like a fear of public speaking are greatly increased. Remember, if you have fun doing something, it is likely you will succeed.

The beginning of a good class typically starts with a general set of course expectations and guidelines. On page 121 there is a sample Course Expectations and Guidelines sheet used in my speech classes. Following a course description, there should be some fun activities to alleviate your fears and anxieties.

Note Card Method of Participation

This activity is an example of a teacher putting students on an even scale of participation. Susan Winebrenner states in her book, *Teaching Kids with Learning Difficulties in the Regular Classroom,* that you participate better if you are selected to perform randomly. The card method of class interaction insures one hundred percent class participation. Sometimes, however, students will want to volunteer and, to a point, volunteering is good, until some students dominate.

According to Winebrenner, the best way to establish a fair ground for student performance is to have the students each write on a note card their first and last names. The teacher mixes the cards up and selects the participants randomly from the stack. Your teacher may keep these handy for constant reference in class discussions, to set up speaker order, or for general review of speaking techniques (24).

Break the Ice with Games

The Card Game

This game is a great way to have fun and get to know your classmates. My high school teacher and friend Gary Addington, speech teacher and debate coach for over thirty years, created this exercise. In this game you write your name on a card or you use the cards you may have created for your teacher. You include five things about yourself on the card and pin your card to your shirt. You then get up from your seat and roam around to read the names of other students. After about thirty seconds, you all return to your seats to write down the names and things you can remember. You will have about two minutes to write things down. You repeat this process several more times, or at least until it appears that most of you know the majority of your classmates. Once one student can name all of his or her classmates, the game is over and that student has won.

Nonverbal Game of Human Communications

Another great first-day activity coming from the Addington archives is a nonverbal game in human communications. This game requires hardy volunteers. Two or three student volunteers leave the classroom. The volunteers will be called in one at a time. While they are out of the room, the class selects a place in the room where the student is supposed to go. The students all clap once in unison when the volunteer enters the room. For each step the volunteer takes towards the target area, the students clap once in unison. When the volunteer moves away from the target, the students remain still. Sometimes the volunteer never finds the target — the game should be stopped once it is apparent the volunteer has reached a maximum frustration level. Then, the next volunteer comes in. Volunteers need to be those who appear resilient.

Liar

This game is found in Brent Oberg's book, *Speechcraft*. In this game, everyone in the class gets a few minutes to come up with a story, either true or false. Before presenting the story, the student gives the teacher a small piece of paper indicating whether their story is T for true or F for false. The student presents his or her story. The object of the game is to trick as many students as possible. After the story, the students vote on how many believe the story to be true or false. The student who read the story writes on the board the number of those who believe the story and those who think it is a lie. If the story is true and fifteen students think it is a lie and ten believe it is true, then the student writes plus five on the board (32-3).

Um

This game is simple and you learn fluency from it. The students are given an easy topic like those listed below. Each student gets up and speaks on the topic until he or she utters a dreaded verbal pause like "um," "and like," "ah," "uh," or any other filler.

Sample Topics

Fingers, summer, winter, trips, airplanes, chick flicks, boring classes, a bad date, baseball, sumo wrestling, ballet, good literature, sushi, computers, board games, important dates, holidays, happiness, the dentist, perfume, grass, trees, football, fans, weddings, graduation, papers, good grades, typing, soccer, the prom, midnight, news, gossip, teachers, police, trouble, cars, insurance, cliques, basketball, school dances, nail polish, flying saucers, Frisbees, etc.

Question Dialogue Game

You first get a partner and then the teacher will give you a situation, maybe from the list below. Then you ask questions to each other while moving the conversation along. When one can no longer continue the stream of questions, another student replaces that person. Change the situation and continue in the same manner.

An easy variation of this game is playing Freeze Frame, where two students act out a certain situation until someone from the class yells out "freeze" and replaces one of the pair and concocts a new situation.

Sample Situations

Two firemen not too eager to get to a fire. A boss firing an employee. Two people stuck in an elevator. Two people at a movie that one likes and the other hates. Friends planning to go out. Policemen trying to avoid the scene of a crime. Teachers not in a hurry to get to class. The dentist talking to a patient about accidentally pulling the wrong tooth. A tennis player arguing with the linesperson about a missed call. An agent telling the client that the client is over the hill and worthless. Two pilots wondering how to fly the plane now that the automatic pilot does not work. A parent catching a child sneaking out after curfew. Policemen fighting over a doughnut. Teachers arguing over who needs to pay more for a shared meal at a restaurant. A psychiatrist and a patient. A sportscaster interviewing an athlete. A host and celebrity interview. On-the-scene reporter and eyewitness. A police detective and suspect interrogation. Lawyer talking to a witness. A politician being interviewed by a reporter. Any fictional character and talk show host.

Nonsense

Another game is for you to speak nonsense to a partner in a given situation. Like the Question Dialogue Game above, you act out situations where you speak, but you simply talk gibberish. You get several minutes to figure out how you are going to act it out.

Sample Situations

Two thieves planning a break in. People stuck in an elevator. A waiter giving the wrong food to a couple. Getting pulled over for speeding. Getting yelled at by the principal. One person translating poetry for another in a different language. One person winning an Academy Award. A judge passing down a guilty sentence. Being caught for shoplifting in a store. Getting caught drinking by a parent. Sneaking home after curfew and getting caught. A couple buying a car and one likes it and the other doesn't. A couple watching a movie at a theatre and one likes the movie and the other wants to leave.

Chapter Two:
Self-Introduction Speeches

There are three types of self-introductory speeches covered in this chapter: the 3-D Collage, Self-Presentation Introductory Speech, and the Interview Activity.

The 3-D Collage

This assignment is largely adapted from Gary Addington's regular course. The 3-D Collage is a great way for you to introduce yourself to the class. Typically, the teacher will give the class a three- to four-minute presentation on him or herself to model the activity. This section goes into great detail over the 3-D Collage because it covers a variety of learner objectives and outcomes.

The 3-D Collage is a great way for you to disclose information about yourself through a medium of visual presentation where you create an actual representation of yourself and explain how what you created is much like you.

Examples of the 3-D Collage

A student could create a Yin and Yang out of Styrofoam to show the differences in things that he or she likes and does. In the center of one could be a variety of representations of things he or she enjoys, like a camera to show interest in photography. While in the center of the other, he or she might place work stubs, report cards, and other things that represent the responsibilities he or she may have.

One student could create a mountain out of clay and basically explain how life is like a mountain. He or she could go on to extend the metaphor by saying how getting through school is like climbing a mountain. He or she might love to ski and includes a pair of tiny skis, which are easy to get at a local Hobby Lobby or specialty hardware store. He or she places representations on the model and brings in things to assist in explaining about his or her life.

Another student could illustrate how life is like a book with various chapters. He or she brings a homemade book and displays pictures and points out how various pieces of his or her life make up chapters. He or she can extend the metaphor further by pointing out how incidents in his or her life are like the plot summary of a story: setting, rising action, climax, falling action, and denouement. Of course, there is no requirement for you to follow that specific a regimen.

Students have created mobiles of all sorts to show how life is a series of balances. They put all kinds of things on them that illustrate the various facets of their lives.

Students can create model computers to show the extent of their technological interests. They put things into the computer, and during their presentation, they take symbols out of their computer that represent aspects of their lives.

One student explained how her life is like a painter's palette, instead of paint, she put items that symbolized aspects of her life. Another student created a large Styrofoam puzzle with pieces representing parts of her life.

My own collage includes "All My World's a Stage" where there was a small stage and a tiny student's desk on it with a variety of other representations for my life. Another collage I did was the metaphor "Life is a Voyage" with an old globe depicting places I have been with representations pinned onto the globe. You will come up with your own ideas.

For a sample assignment sheet and rubric for the 3-D Collage, see page 122.

Self-Presentation Introductory Speech

This type of introduction speech is more straightforward and less complicated than the 3-D Collage. Another gem from Brent Oberg's *Speechcraft* is to give a speech designed to introduce yourself to the class. You can present the speech from a different point of view. For example, you could present the speech from the point of view of a minister eulogizing you in a speech about the various parts of your life. You could present the speech from the viewpoint of a best friend. You could even present from the point of view of a beloved pet. This assignment should be between three to four minutes. As in all introductory speeches, you can introduce many aspects of your life: family, hobbies, sports, favorite subjects, TV shows, and other influences (14).

The Interview Activity

The purpose of this project, like the 3-D Collage and the Self-Presentation Introductory Speech, is to introduce yourself to your classmates. Here, you will work in pairs. This activity is a good way to share the burden from one student presenting to one being helped by an interviewer. After one student interviews the other, the roles are reversed.

The interviewer needs to develop a skill to control a conversation. One way to start is to look at the dynamic of the interview. Here are some questions for the interviewer to ask him or herself before working on the actual interview: What is the purpose of the interview? What makes a good interview? How can a response be elicited? What are the interviewer's motivations? Motivation is important to note because an employer conducting an interview to hire someone has different motivation than a news reporter asking a witness questions about a story.

Your Mission

This interview seeks to introduce the subject (person being interviewed) to the class. Ask about a student's hobbies, family life, and general information. A provocative question includes finding out more than just superficial information about the subject. Beyond the usual queries of general information, students could ask whether or not the subject participates in extracurricular activities. Sample questions could be: What are your social outlets? What channels do you use to connect socially? (Examples could be church, Mosque, Temple, youth group, sports team, mall, telephone, etc.) Are you consistent in your behavior? Do you feel bored sometimes or never? Are you often lazy, sometimes or never? Do you have any pets? Do you take care of your pet? What are your favorite movies? What do you like about music, the lyrics or the melody? Do you belong to any groups outside of school? Do you do any volunteer work? If you had a million dollars, how would you spend it? Does an outside force motivate you, or do you motivate yourself? Do you have a favorite superhero? Have you ever been out of the country? Have you had a near-death experience? Do you often travel? What are your goals in life?

Remember to use class time wisely and know your subject has been adequately prepped. Do not ask embarrassing or inappropriate questions. If a question might be inappropriate, it certainly should be left out. For a sample rubric, see page 122.

Chapter Three:
Demonstration Speeches

Your goal with this exercise is to explain to the class how to do something, like how to make a cake or how to play the harmonica. You are to select a topic from the list at the end of this chapter or come up with an original, approved idea of your own. Once you have selected your topic, the library is a good place to go and research information on how to present it. Since these speeches require you to bring in a visual aid, that will make the presentation easier as the visual aid can serve to prompt or remind you of what to say.

You must actively listen to the speaker. On page 123 there is the Student Comment Sheet that shows you how to take notes on your classmates' speeches. In this way you are practicing active listening. Remember, speaking in front of others is challenging and it is important to keep the criticism constructive. Your teacher may choose to give each speaker the criticism from the class, so always remember to keep criticisms constructive. You can use the Student Comment Sheet to help you take notes.

For the Demonstration Speech Scoring Guide, see page 124. There is a Demonstration Speech Worksheet on page 125 that will help you organize your speech.

Main Points for Public Speaking and Delivering Your Demonstration Speech

The purpose of this assignment is to familiarize yourself with refined public speaking. You learn to work with a visual to deliver a demonstration speech, and you work on proper etiquette. The main points of public speaking are the following:

- Eye Contact — The presenter maintains eye contact with the audience by making an attempt to look at everyone. Ideally, even a student in the back of the room should feel connected to the speaker. Vary eye contact to include every part of the room.
- Body Control — The presenter generally keeps feet at shoulder width and does not lean on the podium. The speaker

plans movement at the front of the class. For example, the speaker moves a few steps to the right to illustrate one point and maybe a few steps to the left to show another point. The presenter avoids repetitive movement like pacing or swaying. Often, the presenter may not realize that he or she is pacing or swaying; therefore, it is important to rehearse with a friend.

- Hand Gestures — The presenter varies hand gestures. Keep hand gestures above the waist. Avoid repeating the same gestures. Keep hands at the sides when not using a planned gesture. Coordinate gestures with body position. Avoid hands in pockets, fig-leafed in front, or behind the back. Remember, if you're not sure where to put your hands, keep them casually at your sides.

- Voice Control — Tone, pace, and volume contribute to the quality of the presentation. Tone reflects the pitch. Pace defines the speed at which the presenter speaks. Volume is the loudness or softness in the delivery. It is important to vary the tone of a presentation. Avoid being monotone, for that delivery tends to bore the audience. It is important to realize the speed at which you speak. Usually, the beginning public speaker delivers the speech too rapidly without even realizing the audience has a hard time following. If the speech comes too slowly, the audience may lose interest. Pace needs to be varied as with tone and volume.

- Overall Presence — Delivering a speech is challenging. We all get nervous. Sometimes anxiety can be a positive influence on a speaker. The excitement that one feels shows a positive enthusiasm for the subject that he or she presents. It is important to show an interest in the subject you present. One way to avoid the presence of nervousness in a speech is to prepare by rehearsing your written speech. A few pointers are to take direction notes on the speech. Write down where you might want to pause or where you need to increase volume to add emphasis. The better one prepares, the more comfortable one will deliver the speech.

- Appearance — Dress professionally. The care and thought put into appearance lets the audience know that you take your speech seriously.

Possible Topics for Demonstration Speeches

How to survive in a new school
How to put on makeup
How to dress up
How to meditate
How to make mud pie
How to take a vacation
How to play an instrument
How to prepare a dinner
How to create a cartoon
How to plan for a wedding
How to plan a camping trip
How to climb a mountain
How to play tennis
How to rock climb
How to surf
How to prepare for a bicycle/motorcycle trip
How to change oil and maintain a car
How to eat properly
How to plan a car trip
How to plan a hike
How to take care of equipment
How to do morning calisthenics
How to join a club
How to protest
How to plan a class period
How to make balloon animals
How to stay out of trouble
How to get good grades
How to do hair
How to make a floral arrangement
How to prepare tea
How to run for office
How to get out of a traffic ticket
How to vote
How to support troops serving abroad
How to become an FBI or CIA agent
How to contact your local representative

Visit www.soyouwanna.com for more ideas.

Chapter Four:

Evening News, Sports Broadcasting, and Commercials

Evening News

This is a great activity where you can actually report the news. This broadcasting experience can be fun for you to work with a few of your mates and make a team, working just like a broadcast team does while reporting the news. The newscast reports on a variety of current events and themes. One person can report from the local scene, another member speaks on a national issue, a third participant does sports and entertainment, someone can do weather, etc. Each person must speak for at least one minute. This report can be arranged however the group decides. A great way to organize this activity is to get a newspaper and each of you take a different section.

As mentioned above, you will look at different sections in the newspaper to separate roles. There is an anchor who facilitates roles between reports. The anchor also speaks on the day's top stories. For example, the anchor can provide a preview of what the team will cover like in the news example below.

Another variation is that you can create a school report about what is going on around school. You could report on the various athletic programs along with other school-related activities like choral concerts, band performances, testing dates, etc. Use the Broadcast News Worksheet on page 126 to help organize your thoughts. There is a sample rubric on page 127.

The following is an example of what you could create as a news team.

JIM: Today's news includes trouble in the Middle East, and then we'll go to local news with Marsha reporting on the teacher shortage. And Mike will fill us in on the latest with the power shortage situation. And from our sports desk, Bill explains the continued woes of the Rockies. And now for news from the Middle East where suicide bombers have struck once again.

20

(He speaks more on the topic.) And now to Marsha for our local news and word on the teacher shortage.

MARSHA: Thanks, Jim. The metro area experiences a lack of teachers due to increased numbers of schools and students. *(She speaks more on the topic.)* Back to you, Jim.

JIM: Thanks, Marsha. And now Mike discusses the latest proposal concerning the power shortage.

MIKE: Thanks, Jim. It appears as if the California power outages may affect us locally in the coming weeks. *(He speaks more on the topic.)* Back to you, Jim.

JIM: Well, we'll be sure to keep an eye on those developments. Thanks, Mike. And now it's time for sports, where Bill reports on those pesky Rockies. What's going on with our team, Bill?

BILL: Well, that's hard to say, Jim. Just when you think they've hit rock bottom, they continue to lose miserably. *(He speaks more on the topic.)* Now back to you, Jim.

JIM: And that concludes our report for the night. Join us tomorrow when Marsha will speak on the transportation strike, Mike will look at the military tribunals, and Bill reports on the big game as the Avs face off with the Devils. Thank you, good night.

Sports Broadcast: Play-by-Play

You'll enjoy sports broadcasting by putting yourself in the drama of athletic competition. Whether or not you are a sports fan, this exercise will develop your ability to speak. You can take actual clips from a game and recreate the dialogue, or you can make up your own event.

Here you can work in groups of two to three. You can cover a segment of a game in a sport in which you are very familiar, but it isn't a must. Some students could choose baseball, others may choose an equestrian event or a soccer match. Whatever the activity, there is a strategy to commentating. Usually, there are two announcers. One announcer does the play-by-play and the other adds the color. A third member could provide relative historic data and additional analysis or report from the field.

The play-by-play member describes the action that takes place in minute detail. By contrast, the color announcer points out the specifics of what the players might be feeling as they are confronted with that situation — how the players might anticipate a certain action from their opponents. In all cases, the color announcer has either played the sport at the level being covered or has coached the sport. You do not need to be intimate with the sport you select, just use your imagination. A helpful hint is to create situations where you know there will be opportunities to get the color announcer's opinion on a certain play.

Each presentation should be at least three minutes in length, more if there are more than two people to each group. Generally, the overall presentation is about ninety seconds per person in the group. The presentation should be balanced between the play-by-play reporter and the color announcer. Be sure to fill in the Sports Broadcast Worksheet on page 127 to help you with formulating your ideas. Another idea is to recreate a radio broadcast by putting a barrier between you and the class. You can use a large sheet of construction paper and simulate a play-by-play broadcast, leaving the action in the game to the imagination of your mates. For a sample rubric, see page 127.

Commercials

Making your own commercials is fun. This activity shows you where school meets Madison Avenue — the center of advertising.

First consider your favorite commercials. Ask yourself the following questions: What makes that commercial good? Does a commercial have to be humorous to be good? Did you get the product name? Is there a jingle or catch phrase that the audience would remember? Why is it that some very entertaining commercials don't succeed at getting you to remember their brand name?

You can create your own products with a group. You can present products based on the needs of the audience. Be sure to select your topics appropriately. You can base your ideas on real products. Ideas for products to promote are listed below. Once you have a good product, fill out the Speech Commercial Worksheet on page 128 to help organize your ideas. A sample rubric can be found on page 128.

Additional ideas for commercial products: soft drinks, diapers, bubblegum, hair spray, cleaning supplies, toothpaste, soap, perfume, makeup, breath mints, mouthwash, bug spray, laundry detergent, deodorant, toilet paper, pain reliever, shampoo, coffee collars, etc.

Tips

The commercial should be at least two minutes. You can come up with your own jingles and catch phrases. The commercial can begin with an attention-getting device that can be brought in as a problem and then you can work towards solving it.

Additional considerations: positive and negative consequences for using or not using the product, cost benefit of the product, the desired effect and outcome of the product.

Section Two:
THE BASICS

Chapter Five:
The Vocabulary of Speech and Debate

The power of vocabulary frees the mind. Vocabulary is one of the most important tools that you can learn to enhance communication. No doubt you become more confident and comfortable when you have a way to express yourself. Exposing yourself to more and more words allows you more options in expression. Every arena of study, from speech to biology, has its own unique language. Learning it is a key step to understanding and using the knowledge it offers. What follows is a list of words frequently used in speech and debate.

advantages: the benefits of a particular plan

alliteration: the repetition of consonant sounds in a phrase or passage

assonance: the repetition of vowel sounds within a phrase or passage

attention-getting device: a way to introduce a topic by getting the audience interested in the speech and the content

bittersweet: the ability of a story to evoke humorous and dramatic reactions from the audience

body control: the ability of a speaker to use gestures and movement to enhance a performance

blocking: the planning of staged movements to enhance the interpretation of a piece

case: an argument developed to support one side of an issue

cheating out: an actor facing toward the audience during a performance

charisma: the positive energy or charm possessed by a speaker

clerk or secretary: the person who records the particulars of a congress session

cross examination: a type of policy debate; or the question-and-answer period in a debate

crossfire: the question-answer-question period in a debate

cutting: a piece taken from a larger work that contains dramatic or humorous elements

disadvantages: the problems associated with changing a current policy

duet: a two-person performance

duo interpretation: a two-person performance where the actors achieve a dramatic or humorous effect

evidence: verified information

extra-topical: an argument outside the guidelines of a given topic

harms: the result of a current policy's disastrous consequences

impromptu: a speech delivered on the moment with minimal or no preparation

improvisation: a speech or act delivered on the moment with minimal or no preparation

inherent barrier: a problem with the current system that prevents a positive change from happening

lead-in: the introduction of a quotation by stating the name, source, or situation before presenting the quotation

monologue: a one-person speech either dramatic, humorous, or informative

monotone: speaking without varying volume or tempo

off script: a cutting delivered without a manuscript in hand

on script: a cutting delivered with a manuscript in hand

opponent: the person supporting the negative side of a resolution

pace or tempo: the rate at which a speaker delivers a speech

parallel structure: the repetition of certain phrases within a passage

parliamentary procedure: the organization of a group in a formal setting

parliamentarian: the person who oversees the congress session

plan: a way to solve a problem, often used by the affirmative in policy debate

planks: steps in a plan to solve a problem

policy: the existing mandate or order in question

policy debate: a debate over the change of a certain policy, sometimes called cross-examination debate

postdate: information that is more recent

presiding officer: the person who runs a congress session

prima fascia case: Latin for "on the face" argument that supports one side of an issue

problem-solution speech: a speech that defines a problem and proposes a solution

pro/con speech: a speech that points out advantages and disadvantages to a certain position on an issue

proponent: the person supporting the affirmative side of a topic or resolution

round-table discussion: a discussion over a group of topics by extemporaneous speakers

significance: the result of a policy's disastrous consequences to a large number of people

signposting: a verbal outline that organizes the speech in easy-to-use terminology

status quo: the existing policy

tripartite division: the repetition of phrases into three parts

topicality: an argument that is within the guidelines of a given topic

value debate: a debate over values

verbal pause: using filler words like "um" or "and like" in a speech

Chapter Six:
Listening

> *"It is the disease of not listening, the malady of not marking that I am troubled withal."*
> — Shakespeare

You may ask yourself, "What is the importance of listening in a public speaking class?" Listening is what makes communication worthwhile. Many studies indicate that people spend more time listening than any other communicative activity. Effective listening can mean the difference between success and failure in life. In *Communication Matters,* Randall McCutcheon breaks down the human communication experience, "The average person spends 9 percent of his daily communication time writing, 16 percent reading, 30 percent speaking, and 45 percent listening. Students spend most of their school time listening up to 60 percent" (53). In *Creative Communication,* Fran Tanner states the benefits of effective listening,

"... a responsive audience stimulates the speaker to give his or her best, to go beyond the call of duty. Become a better listener and you'll become a better speaker, for you will be aware of what the listener needs to understand and remember. Become a better listener and you will be in a position to protect yourself from the dishonest speakers in our society ..." (142).

This chapter encourages positive listening habits and how to become a better communicator through improved listening.

If the ability to speak and persuade is a life skill, the importance of listening cannot be overstated. For example, David P. Reynolds, the Chairman of Reynolds Aluminum says, "The ability to communicate and listen effectively are probably the most important skills at a manager's command because all other management skills depend on it" (Franklin and Clark). The skill of listening makes money for American businesses and ultimately creates jobs. In fact, according to many texts, people can listen at about three times the rate that the average person speaks. Therefore, the listener has added time to become even more effective at such a valuable communicative skill.

Unfortunately, there are several pitfalls that hinder effective listening. One is *ambient noise*. That is the noise that occurs within our environment naturally and has a negative effect on our ability to hear what is being said. Again, it is difficult to listen effectively especially when it becomes easy to yield to distractions, such as ambient noise, around us. Sometimes the listener will allow the speaker's appearance to distract from hearing the message. Another pitfall is an inability to listen to difficult subjects. Either it is the listener's boredom, disinterest, or personal bias that leads to the inability to "get" what is being said. A final pitfall to effective listening is to get caught up in a response before allowing the speaker a chance to finish the presentation. Again, realizing that our effectiveness as communicators relies more on our ability to listen than anything else, we ought to recognize that these pitfalls exist and do our best to listen effectively.

Now that we know the problems, what can you do to practice effective listening techniques? One way is to use positive body position to help adapt to the ambient challenge. It is important to realize that listening to what is going on is far more valuable than allowing whatever it is to distract you. Even though we are told to look and act the part when we are speaking, we should not allow ourselves to miss the opportunities presented by the new information just because the presenter does not match our own personal idea of what he or she should look like. We should never let the topic of discussion prevent us from listening and learning. Even if you have a strong political bias, it should not preclude effective listening to opposing viewpoints. In fact, listening to them might help to solidify your previous political or social ideal. Finally, despite the urge to interrupt — and it is a natural urge because we can listen far faster than a speaker can deliver a speech — try to use the listening gap time to your advantage by taking notes. In those notes, you may want to write questions concerning the content of the speech.

The table below illustrates a clear strategy for effective listening.

Technique	Usage	Activity
Think about listening as an activity	What is the speaker's goal? What personal experience do you have with the topic? How can you use the new information?	Demonstration speech listening feedback sheet
Be physically prepared to listen	Are your eyes on the speaker? Is your back straight? Do you have paper and a pen for notes?	Debate flow sheet completion.
Distinguish between facts and opinion	If the statement can be verified, it is a fact. If the statement is a suggestion as to what we should do, possibly based on fact, it is an opinion.	Student congress voting. Demonstration feedback sheet. Debate flow completion with reason for decision.
Listening spare time	Listener has time to infer a variety of information. Any questions for further consideration on the presentation?	Student congress question and answer period. Debate reason for decision.

Activities Associated with Effective Listening

Class Activity 1
Brainstorm occupations where listening is important.

Class Activity 2
A student tells the class the exact route he or she takes to school. After he or she has spoken, the class writes down in as exact detail as possible the student's route.

Class Activity 3
Students take turns reading short newspaper articles and the rest of the class paraphrases the articles.

Class Activity 4

Students name songs that address miscommunication. One example is Paul Simon's "The Sounds of Silence."

Class Activity 5

Students get into pairs. One student reads an editorial or feature article to himself. He then takes the time to identify the author's goal and supporting details. He then reads the article to his partner while the listener writes notes identifying the author's goals and supporting details. Finally, the two compare their findings.

Class Activity 6

The Heckling Speech consists of the students writing a speech on a controversial topic and presenting it while the teacher or another student interrupts the presenter as he or she is speaking. The speaker must stop, answer the question, and continue with the speech (Oberg, 49).

Class Activity 7

This is the classic telephone game. The teacher writes a story on a piece of paper. The first student reads the paper and tries to replicate the story exactly to the next student, and so on. At the end, see what has become of the little story.

Chapter Seven:
Visual Aids

The importance of using visual aids cannot be overstated in a world where society gets much of its stimulus from images. It's not just enough to state facts to get a point across, it is also important to *show* the audience a clear point through a chart or a graph. In the book *The Art of Speaking* by E.F. Elson and Alberta Peck, the authors describe visuals: "this kind of material speaks a language all its own, the language of the eye and it appeals to almost everyone ... seeing is believing" (153).

Although most would agree that visual aids are essential, there are some caveats. For example, Howard Martin and William Colburn in their book, *Communication and Consensus,* state: "A final kind of nonverbal material that may pose problems is so-called visual aids, such as pictures, graphs, charts, films, and television clips" (109). The dilemma here is that sometimes visual aids tend to distract rather than enhance a presentation. This section explores the positive uses of visual aids and provides some tips for how to be effective with visuals.

As a teacher, I use a wide variety of visual aids: handouts, PowerPoint presentations, the blackboard, overheads, posters, Wikipages, blogs, webcasts, podcasts, charts, graphs, etc. You can use visuals to help you explain your topic.

In her book *Creative Communication,* Fran Tanner provides six suggestions for the use of visual aids:

1. Choose aids that relate directly to your speech. If your purpose is to show the audience how to cast with a fly rod, bring the rod — it relates to your speech. Leave the trolling rod at home — it doesn't relate.

2. Carefully plan your displays ahead of time and rehearse with them. Be sure you have everything you need and that the material is in correct sequence. If you are using electrical equipment, check to see that it works properly. Will you need an extension cord, masking tape for mounting posters, or a pointer for diagrams?

3. Keep your aids clear and simple. In drawings, use wide, heavy lines on large poster board. Use color when possible. Omit

unnecessary details. If it takes more time to explain your aid than it would to explain your point, don't use the aid. Aids should be self-explanatory.

4. Display your visual aids at the proper time. Keep them covered until you need them. Otherwise, they will prove distracting, with the audience wondering what that thing is, instead of listening to you.

5. When using your aid, keep it visible. Stand well to one side as you point to it. Choose or draw material that is large enough for all to see readily. Hold up smaller objects in such a way that your hands do not cover them.

6. Don't fidget with your aids. Use them and then put them aside. Avoid holding them throughout your speech (129).

The most important thing about the use of visuals in a presentation is that you give the audience a clear view as to what you are saying. The visual serves to underscore the message. You are ultimately the best visual aid and what aids you bring to the presentation should help.

If you use graphs and charts, remember a pie graph is great when you are showing components that make up a whole. For example, if you want to show what percentage of the school budget goes toward materials, a pie graph works well. A chart in the form of a bar or line graph works well when you want to show trends in a category. For example, compare car sales from year to year in the fall as opposed to mixing seasons.

Chapter Eight:
Nonverbal Communication

Directly tied to the use of visual aids in speech is nonverbal communication. This form of "wordless" communication extends beyond borders, races, and religions. Some forms of nonverbal communication have already been discussed. (See Demonstration Speeches on page 17.) The rate, pitch, and volume of your voice are forms of auditory nonverbal communications, while hand gestures and body control provide examples of visual nonverbal communications. Much is communicated long before a word is spoken. Although nonverbal communication exists in sports, international understanding, and cultural bias, the primary focus here will be to concentrate on audience and speaker nonverbal cues.

Since some aspects of nonverbal communication exist whenever we meet someone, this silent form of communication can become a great asset to the speaker. The one angle of speech that we all control is our attitude. In fact, throughout life, attitude is the only thing that we uniformly control one hundred percent of the time. An excited, enthusiastic speaker promotes more by presence alone than the content of the speech. In his text *Effective Communication for Today*, Jack Hulbert illustrates the overall importance of nonverbal communication, "your body language may reveal whether you agree or disagree, whether you're enthusiastic or uninterested, or whether you're relaxed or tense" (24). The impact of how a presenter carries him or herself has a distinct bearing on how well the audience receives him or her. In the text *The Essentials of Speech Communication* by Sharon Franklin and Deborah Clark, they cite that "sixty-five percent of a speaker's message is communicated through nonverbal behavior, or body language" (311). Additionally, the same source cites a study conducted by Allen Monroe that audiences respond mostly to eye contact, a pleasing voice, and physical movement: "six important nonverbal aspects to personal delivery — appearance, facial expressions, voice, pauses, eye contact, and gestures and movement" (312). Appearance is the very first thing people see. It certainly makes a difference to an audience. People should dress to the part. A football coach might dress differently as a keynote speaker at an awards banquet than he would in the locker room to address his team before a big game. Facial expressions give the audience a feel for the speaker's enthusiasm. As mentioned during the section on Demonstration Speeches, eye contact serves to include as many audience members as possible. Another key aspect to nonverbal communication is the use of varied voice patterns to keep the audience interested. Is an audience going to enjoy someone who speaks continuously in a monotone? It is important to vary the rate, tone, and volume at which the speech is delivered.

Body control is another great way to attract an audience. All hand gestures need to be above the waist. Remember, you are not presenting to a group of fleas on the ground or to some cosmic aliens in space. Gestures should be varied.

Things to avoid:

1. Repetitive hand gestures distract from what is being said.

2. Avoid swaying. If you know you have a problem swaying, just put your feet close together. If you start to sway, you will tip over. This works as a reminder that you sway. Once the swaying problem is remedied, the speaker should keep feet at shoulder width.

3. Make gestures smooth and even. Avoid being too choppy with your arms and hands.

4. Don't stay in the same place for too long. Try to move around the room to include more of your audience. Plan the movement to coincide with segments of the speech. Don't just move for movement's sake.

Other important nonverbal indicators exist in everyday interpersonal communication. The most powerful international gesture of goodwill is the smile. By far, the smile is the most powerful nonverbal signal around. Another positive nonverbal signal used in everyday communication is the nod. In the text *Communication Matters*, the authors state, "research has shown that applicants who nod during job interviews are hired more often than those who do not" (96). A good strategy for students is to look at the teacher and nod during class. The positive reinforcement helps the student establish positive rapport with the teacher without talking.

The art of nonverbal communication is far-reaching and varied. There are many aspects concerning this part of speech and communications to delve into. On a daily basis, an observer can sometimes tell if someone likes his or her job just by the way he or she goes about the daily routine.

To conclude this section on nonverbal communication, it is apparent that every day you can see how people communicate without having to talk. The power of nonverbal communication reveals within it messages that may be unintended but are understood. Too often in sports participants lose momentum and a lack of enthusiasm is apparent. Heads are down and body language is slouched and negative. A coach can direct them to "keep your head up." This phrase is more than a mere expression when coupled with "look at each other" or "look at me." The very act of looking at someone necessitates the players to pick up their heads and their posture.

Chapter Nine:
Group Dynamics

In a good or successful discussion, members bring all sides of a problem to the surface for consideration. Another positive aspect to group work is the increased level of commitment among members in a group. In his text *Speech Communication and Human Interaction,* Thomas Scheidel notes, "if an individual has participated in and has been able to express his view during decision making by a group, he will then be more committed to the group's final decision, even if it does not represent his personal or original view" (268). Therefore, it is important for you to respect the opinions of others while carefully considering your own contributions to the group efforts. The goal here is for your group to experience the power of *groupthink.* Groupthink is the idea that member interaction as individuals in a group leads to a dynamic and growing form of communication that cannot be duplicated individually.

In politics and in business, the advantages to working within a small group are the foundation of modern day society. One needs go no further than the Communist Revolution to understand that a small group headed by Trotsky and Lenin led to one of the most far-reaching and important movements in modern history: the advent of communism. No matter what one's opinion is concerning this political concept, the fact that it was espoused by more than a billion people in the world undeniably makes it a significant world trend. Hitler started Nazi Germany with a small band of individuals in a Bavarian beer hall. Unfortunately, there was not a small group powerful enough to stop Hitler's insanity. Indeed, the power of the small group dynamic is ubiquitous.

The business world also has numerous important examples. Who would guess that two engineers would collaborate to make one of the world's best-selling computers and calculators? Enter Hewlett and Packard. What would be less likely than two college dropouts developing what would become the world's largest corporation? Steven Jobs and Bill Gates founded the basis for Microsoft. When considering these political and business precedents, the power of the group dynamic is worthy to consider.

There are a couple of different types of small group orientation and discussion. One is the small group discussion. The authors of the book *The Art of Speaking* point out some distinctions, "Small group discussion falls mostly into the category of what is called round-table discussion, and large group discussion is generally identified with the forum or open forum ... "(Elson and Peck, 338). How can small groups help you to learn the art of public speaking? The key to answering this question is to take your group responsibilities seriously. It is important to contribute effectively to your group while respecting and integrating the contributions of others.

One good thing you'll enjoy about group work is that it provides you with relief from the age-old lecture-test format. The challenge for you is to agree as a group to stay on task. As you read through this book, you will see that several assignments loan themselves to group work. Choral Reading, Evening News, and group debates are examples of group assignments.

Leadership Style

On an individual level, all of you need to take advantage of the opportunity to lead the class and develop a leadership style. The student congress is one example that provides a chance for leadership with its format of one person controlling the class in the form of a presiding officer. Even if not all of you have the chance to lead a student congress by fulfilling the role of presiding officer, you all take the floor and give speeches, your mates ask and answer questions about a certain issue, and they lobby the class for or against legislation. The congress session gives you a chance to develop your leadership style. Take a look at the following model of leadership styles largely adapted from Rudolph Verderber's text, *Speech for Effective Communication*. This model is coupled with class activities that display where you practice certain types of leadership in class (459).

tyle	Description	Advantages	Problems	Where in class?
Laissez-faire or Nondirective Leadership	Responsibilities are shared by all group members	Works well if several members can lead discussions	Guidance must come from within the group	Choral Reading, debate over the issues, news broadcasting
Authoritarian or Directive Leadership	One person leads	Works well if time is limited and instruction concise	Too much power in the hands of too few	Student congress, round-table format
Democratic or Supportive Leadership	Class collaborates on assignments	Works well if all contribute	Is ineffective if not enough contribute	Demonstration Speeches, 3-D Collages

During Demonstration Speeches, you are often paired to work together as a means of helping to rehearse and organize speeches. One person may take the instructions and the rubric while another one speaks. The listener works with the materials to make sure the presenter is following the rules.

During Choral Reading, you divide and organize yourselves so as to come up with a viable interpretive performance. The roles in the interpretive event may not be specified as clearly as in a group debate, but the fact that everyone must work as a unit to fulfill the obligations of the assignment gives you the opportunity to develop your own niche within the group. The group debate has an easy-to-follow group dynamic. Groups can be organized within the constructs of the debate itself. One person is responsible for the introduction, the next for the cross-examination, one for rebuttal, and so on.

Fortunately, in the world of speech and debate, many group dynamics are pre-constructed within the parameters of any given assignment. An equal contribution from all members is the instructor's primary challenge. Many activities have a group dynamic already built into the assignment, allowing students to easily see the different roles. Student congress provides opportunities for students to find their leadership styles in a variety of ways. Overall class leadership is evident through the running of classes as the presiding officer. Tactical leadership occurs when students take the floor to introduce and debate legislation. When these ideas on group dynamics are learned early on, you get a feel for group dynamics, preparing you for assignments that allow you to work more closely with other groups on subsequent projects.

Chapter Ten:

Transitions and Verb Activation

Transitions and Linking Expressions

A *transition* is a word or group of words designed to give a reader or listener some obvious directional signals. Transitions act like thread that sews your ideas together. They explain how one idea is linked to another. Transitions show a definite chronology and will help you improve your writing. The following is adapted from a list given to me by Charles Lettes, a former colleague and dear friend. Keep this list — students have often come to me for a copy years after they have graduated.

Transitions for Narration – Time Transitions

after	before
later	then
in the meantime	afterwards
during	meanwhile
until	today
as	finally
next	when
at the same time	first
now	while

Transitions for Description

above	below
in the distance	overhead
across from	beyond
nearby	on my left (right)
also	further
next to	opposite to
before me	here
over	to the left (right)

Transitions for Adding to Ideas Already Stated

again	besides
For instance	Moreover
also	Finally
Furthermore	One example of
another	First ... second ...
In addition	Another example of
at the same time	such
likewise	similarly
equally important	For example
too	In concert with
Whereas	

Transitions for Showing Result – Cause and Effect Relationships

accordingly	because
Therefore	As a result
Consequently	thus
at last	hence
To sum up	At this point
since	Whereas

Transitions for Contrasting Ideas

Although	On the one hand
On the contrary	Conversely
but on the other hand	Contrary to
In opposition to	However
otherwise	while
in contrast	Nevertheless
still	yet

Note: Capitalized transitions often begin a sentence.

Verb Activation

In my career I have been blessed with excellent colleagues. Kent Sauls gave me the following idea and I gladly pass it along to you. As with transitions, verb activation improves your word selection and will benefit your ability to speak and to write.

Helping Verbs – a.k.a Auxiliary Verbs

is	do
are	did
was	does
were	may
have	might
has	can
had	would
be	should
been	shall
being	will
am	could

Helping Verb Combinations

will be	should have
shall be	would have
could be	must have
have been	should have been
had been	could have been
has been	must have been

Present Tense Verbs in the Active Voice

Using these verbs or verbs like them improves communication skills. For example, the sentence, "It is good for them" can be activated to "It benefits them."

reveals	describes
defines	reasons (that)
presents	expostulates (on)
constructs (in place of "makes")	emerges
discusses (in place of "says")	develops
explains	grows
emphasizes	benefits
upholds	implies (that)
enlarge (in place of "make bigger")	proposes
writes	widen
proves	deepen

Chapter Eleven:
Cutting Drama and Humor

In addition to the public speaking events in Section Three are the interpretive events. Your main challenge with these particular events is the selection of materials. Interpreting and cutting humor and drama for an eight- to ten-minute performance takes effort in finding and reading fresh material, then making the cutting from the entire work. In this chapter there will be four descriptions of outstanding cuttings delivered from the 2002 Charlotte Queen City National Tournament. Two selections are from humorous interpretation and two are from dramatic performances.

Cutting for Humor

The development of humorous interpretation from prose, poetry, or dramatic literature requires several steps. The first one is to read the material at hand. Additionally, looking for instances of verbal irony or slapstick within the reading becomes essential. Finally, it becomes important for you to integrate the specific selections in order to come up with a finished product. Therefore, a completed cutting includes the following: a teaser (short attention-getting selection from the target piece), an introduction explaining the scenes and author, and the cutting itself. The cutting follows the story line to some degree, but your job is to create a tale in the cutting itself. The parameters for a cutting as required by the National Forensic League maintain that a piece must be published in book form with an ISBN.

Initially, a book or play is usually selected. In most instances, plays make for the best type of cutting because they are created to be dramatized. At this point, it is important to read the target literature. Typically, one can look to instances of humor and highlight them in the text, or copy the page then highlight that selection from within the page. Instances need to be encased in scenes in order to make sense. Even if the whole concept of the piece is nonsensical, there needs to be adequate background and information given in the piece to establish some sort of continuity. The cutting may consist of just one scene lasting from eight to ten minutes. Or, the cutting may take parts of several scenes to encapsulate a story. Once pages are copied and selections identified, you select a chronology — this sequence does not necessarily reflect the book order. In other words, there is room to rearrange scenes. Then you cut out the selections and paste them to letter-sized sheets of construction paper to assist in memorizing. Again, the loyalty remains more with the cutting than the author. Yet, the writer originates the ideas and the scenes performed in the piece.

Thus, the challenge in cutting the piece becomes the creation of a humorous cutting that contains the funny parts along with a recognizable background. One way to meet this test is to read conscientiously and to look for a variety of humorous elements. Satires, irony, farce, slapstick, and hyperbole are good indicators of humorous material. It is important to read the material carefully at the beginning to assess the possibility of material to cut for humor. Another difficult aspect of the process becomes the selection and assessment of materials arranged together to tell a tale. The placement of scenes to create an effective piece works to create the artistic unity of a smaller piece within the larger novel or play.

The nuts and bolts of the cutting of humorous literature exist in some actual cuttings. At the 2002 NFL National Tournament at Charlotte, North Carolina, I witnessed several humorous interpretations. To make it to nationals, one must win his or her district competition. Depending on the depth of competition, these district qualification tournaments represent exceptional talent. The national tournament displays the best of the best. At all levels of competition, there are many examples of humorous interpretation. The following are two of the better pieces.

All about Al by Cherie Vogelstein promotes the situational irony of who is really sane.

The teaser begins:

Voice One: How are you?

Voice Two: I'm suicidal.

Voice One: Yeah, so I heard.

Introduction: Tells of a man about to split with his girlfriend in a coffee house when he unexpectedly sees his insane friend Al. The intro also identifies the piece and the author.

The cutting resumes with the material. The sane guy and Al continue to discuss why the former wants out of a great relationship with a great lady. The sane one does not want Al around to hear the conversation when his soon-to-be ex-girlfriend shows up. Al has the sane guy explain what the problem is exactly. They create a humorous role-play with Al being the woman. The cutting ends with the sane guy realizing that he was about to break up with the best girl in the world.

The humor in this piece comes from the situational irony and hyperbole in that the sane guy learns from his insane friend, Al, how to deal with potentially the rest of his life, while Al may commit suicide at any instant.

Linin' Fat by Judi Ann Mason intertwines the teaser with an introduction where the performer can show a wide array of voices, while stereotyping the characters portrayed throughout the cutting.

The story starts when the janitor of a bank finds money after his bank has been robbed. The janitor has a wife, children, and in-laws. Each of them has an idea about what to do with the money. The whole time characters live out a stereotyped existence with their desires on the money. Meanwhile, there is the moral question of returning the money. In the end, the mother threw out old linens to make room for their new, improved lifestyle. Unfortunately, the money was kept in a pillowcase that had just been tossed.

The humor in this selection emanates from the stereotyping of middle class African Americans. Also, the ironic twist in the end that making way for the new and improved lifestyle of relative wealth creates the motivation to clean out the old pillowcase, which contains the family's new means. Another source of humor in this piece was the answer to the question of "What role does morality play in the face of such obvious gains?"

Humorous cutting of literature contains a variety of philosophies. Currently, it is accepted practice to alter the script so as to achieve smooth transitions in a selection. However, to promote the existence of "The Back Street Boys" in a Shel Silverstein piece goes beyond what is acceptable revision. The reason is that Silverstein wrote his works before the Backstreet Boys existed. You need to realize that creating an honest, fresh cutting is of greater value than criminally plagiarizing a cutting.

Cutting for Drama

Much like the humorous interpretive piece, the cutting of a dramatic piece relies on reading and selecting the dramatic parts of a given work of literature. The first step is the student's reading of the piece. As a reader, you look for scenes from within the piece to make an eight- to ten-minute dramatic performance. A primary difference between dramatic and humorous interpretation is the presence of dramatic tension. Often, good pieces will incorporate elements of both drama and humor to strengthen the overall effect of the cutting. In this section, you will look at the specifics of "what to cut" to strengthen a piece. Finally, we will examine how the objectives of quality drama are met in a pair of selections from the 2002 Charlotte National Forensic League Tournament final round.

Much like the cutting of a humorous piece, the dramatic selection incorporates reading and marking possible selections for a cutting as you read. One key to marking selections is to find elements of conflict within dialogue. Dramatic and verbal irony are viable literary features to set up a dramatic piece. These sections deliver passion through drama. As with any interpretive piece, continuity is an essential element in creating a believable piece.

Once the play or novel is read, you can photocopy the pages with the selection and create the context for a cutting. As with humorous interpretation, you can rearrange the chronology to assist in the creation of a story-within-a-story cutting. This progression follows the same steps as the humorous interpretation. Additionally, this type of performance is for one person.

In order to read and cut a selection, a solid work ethic emerges as a constant in your success as a performer. The willingness to read several plays and make decisions as to which ones are worth cutting will only work if you have the self-motivation to read and track the cuttings. One way to show the rewards of hard work is through modeling that behavior to achieve results.

Before continuing with the examination of national finalist drama pieces, you must understand that hard work is not always respected. What if you have the work ethic and do not achieve the results? Three factors influencing success at a speech tournament need to be discussed here. The judge may have individual preferences or biases that may preclude the success of a certain genre. The second factor is that competition is randomly selected. In other words, you could face the toughest competitors in the beginning of the tournament and be knocked out of final round consideration. The third factor is the work ethic. If you show that you are familiar and practiced with the selection, then you will have a comparative advantage over students who are not as well prepared. Of the three factors, the only one you have control over is work ethic. Another problem exists when you may have the work ethic and still have difficulties achieving respect. In this case, other influences such as age or natural ability can inhibit you from succeeding.

The following two pieces are among "the best of the best" in 2002.

In *Shakespeare for my Father* by Lynn Redgrave, the teaser places a small girl in front of an omnipotent king. At the end of the teaser, it becomes clear that the king is the girl's father.

The introduction presents the Redgrave family as having difficulties in communicating and even knowing each other as a family.

The cutting continues to explore the relationship between the father and daughter all the while maintaining the "father as king" metaphor. The aspect of unrealized expectations from the father's perspective pervades the daughter's psyche to a nightmarish point.

In *Lady Day at Emerson's Bar* by Lanie Robertson, the teaser begins with a blues song, and immediately, one has the sense of another Billie Holiday piece. The introduction continues with the character information.

The piece becomes a monologue of Billie Holiday's memories and things she had to go through in the Jim Crow era of America. She starts washing dishes at a whorehouse and continues through her emergence as a great singer, yet not allowed to use the restrooms at one of the USO show venues. The piece ends with her admission of guilt to drug offenses for which she may have been framed.

Both of these pieces succeed for a few reasons. They are both cut very well, transitions were clear, and the audience knew exactly where the story was going. Both students use voice inflections and strategic, well-planned pauses to capture the attention of the audience. The use of metaphor in the first piece definitely allows the listener to read into the piece beyond literal interpretation. The fact that these competitors worked hard to polish these pieces is evident.

These pieces represent the absolute pinnacle of dramatic performance.

Chapter Twelve:
Basic Debate

Welcome to the world of debate where you will learn to logically formulate ideas. When you begin, you need to understand that this form of organized debate is different from arguing with your brother or sister over who is going to wash the dishes. In fact, if you have participated in a student congress, you have already learned one form of debate. There are several different types of debate you can learn, and four are covered in this chapter.

Brainstorming is a great way to come up with topics for the four types of debates being covered in this chapter. You state these topics in the form of a "Resolved that" statement. Therefore, when you write topics you start with the words "Resolved that" and think about topics you would want to debate. You put your decided topic in the "Resolved that" form.

The Class Debate

The class debate is where all students take a side. The topic is stated in the form of a resolution. For example, you could discuss the issues of a porous border between the U.S. and Mexico. The resolution could look something like this: Resolved that the U.S. more strictly enforce border laws. Students who want to speak for this resolution should align themselves on the same side of the room. Students who are against this resolution should be on the opposite side of the room.

The goal is for a student from each side to present a reason for his or her position. It is important that you take turns. After one side has presented an argument, the other side gets to refute that argument. If one side asks a question, the other side responds. This type of debate can go on until arguments are exhausted. It is important that each student respects the speaker. Also, it is important that the speaker not dominate the debate by speaking too much. If you have spoken already, try to allow others in your group to participate. If you are shy by nature, try to take some initiative and contribute to the debate.

Depending on the situation, you may be asked to brainstorm your arguments before the actual debate. You can distribute certain points to team members — those on the same side. You may also want to anticipate the other side and refute their arguments. The teacher can declare a winner, or others can be assigned the task of judging and state reasons for a decision.

The Three-Group Debate

The next form of debate is also class-oriented. As with the class debate mentioned above, each side sits together. Only this time, there is a third group who is undecided. This group sits in the middle. The format works very much the same as the class debate. Each side presents arguments one at a time, allowing the other side to respond to the arguments and come up with their own points. The difference in this debate is that the students in the middle move to the side that persuades them. The debate winner is the side who convinces more of the middle group.

Debate over the Issues

Another more formal type of debate is where you break up into several groups based on interest concerning a variety of issues. Then each group comes up with a "Resolved that" statement that can be argued. You may need to be assigned a side. Even if it goes against your personal opinion, it is important to practice the art of debate; you may become more familiar with persuasive techniques by working against your own opinion. It is important to practice the skill of supporting research as the desired outcome of this activity. Once topics are selected and you are in a group, you are ready to research. Go to the library to gather important information on your topic.

The questioning period is the next aspect of the debate that students really enjoy. They like having their preparation put to the test by their peers. Remember that the point of the questions should not be to make the opposing team look bad. The point should be to clarify the arguments of the opposition.

The final aspect of this debate is the rebuttal. This is the most challenging aspect of the debate because you have to respond to what the opponent has said. Remember to match up what is said to logical refutation. The rebuttal merely extends existing arguments; no new arguments should be presented. New research that bolsters existing arguments is acceptable. This is where your research anticipating the opposition should pay off.

You will have some prep time to help you formulate responses to arguments you have just heard. The best use of prep time probably comes either before the questioning period or before the rebuttal. You will get about two to three minutes per side for prep time. You should definitely take notes on your opponent's speeches. Even if you are listening, you will also take notes, or flow the debate to determine a winner.

A Strategy for Taking Notes During the Debate

On your own paper, draw a large box divided into four sections. One box is for notes on affirmative opening remarks and the box next to that is for notes on negative opening remarks. The box below the notes on the affirmative opening remarks is for notes on the affirmative rebuttal, and the box next to that is for notes on the negative rebuttal. Then write your *reason for decision* or RFD. Explain why you think the affirmative or negative team won.

Debate over the Issues Explanation

The format of the debate for four students, two on each side, should look like this:

Four-minute affirmative speech: students proposing or supporting the issue.

Two-minute cross-examination period by the negative: students negate the issue; the questioning period seeks to clarify points as opposed to simply arguing against the other side.

Four-minute negative speech: students present against the resolution for two minutes and attack the affirmative case for the remaining two minutes. Remember, bring up what the affirmative has stated and why their contentions do not work.

Two-minute affirmative cross-examination period by the affirmative: students affirm the issue; the questioning period seeks to clarify points as opposed to simply arguing against the other side.

Two-minute negative rebuttal: bring up the affirmative position and why it does not work. Explain why the proposal would not be a good idea, giving the negative team the victory. In other words, explain why the negative wins the debate.

Two-minute affirmative rebuttal: bring up the initial affirmative position, the negative attacks against it, and why the affirmative should win the debate. Why is the proposal a good idea?

Hint: When you speak, you can organize your speech in an outline format. For example, you can state a reason as *Point One* and evidences as to why this reason works as *Subpoint A,* and so on. This type of format makes it easy for the opponent and the audience to refer to specific points.

For a sample rubric, see Grading Criteria for Debate over the Issues on page 129.

Public Forum Debate Format

Topics are selected monthly by the National Forensic League. You can find the topic on nflonline.org under the "Resources" tab and then select "Topics." Find the "Public Forum" subheading and you'll find lots of topics. You can also make up your own topic.

The coin toss winner may choose either affirmative or negative, or first or second speaker. For example, if a team selects affirmative or negative, then the opposing side can select first or second speaker. If the team selects first or second speaker, then the opposing side selects affirmative or negative.

On pages 130 and 131 are two forms to aid you in this debate. The Public Forum Worksheet will help you organize your points for debate. The Flow Sheet for Public Forum Debate will help you as an audience member to take notes on the debate and decide a winner.

Time Limits

Each side gets two minutes of preparation.
Team A Speaker 1 – four minutes
Team B Speaker 1 – four minutes
Crossfire between A1 and B1 – three minutes
Team A Speaker 2 – four minutes
Team B Speaker 2 – four minutes
Crossfire between A2 and B2 – three minutes
A1 Summary – two minutes
B1 Summary – two minutes
Grand Crossfire between all speakers – three minutes
A2 Last Shot – one minute
B2 Last Shot – one minute

Helpful Hints

Develop arguments using signposting language so the audience can see where you are going.

A debater will want to use two to four central ideas to base his or her case:

1. A historical perspective as a means to avoid repeating the past is a viable strategy. For example, the U.S. could support the Strategic Defense Initiative (Star Wars) by stating how weak the French, British, and other allies were during 1938 and 1939, before the Nazi invasion of Western Europe. The conclusion being that they were weak due to a lack of preparation.

2. Philosophical case arguments could be used. For example, if liberty is more important than security or justice, one could use freedom as a central idea.

3. Real world arguments state the way things are. Despite the fact that something in our world is undesirable, in order to succeed in changing it, we have to accept what it is before we can make it better. For example, it might be that minorities still make less money, but until the real world causes are identified, we could never change that issue.

4. The most compelling and difficult central idea could be economic reasoning. Usually the appeal to a judge is that the cost drives the right decision. If the topic calls for admitting more members into NAFTA, for example, the affirmative could argue that increased exports create more jobs. Conversely, the negative could stipulate a study showing that the U.S. would lose some jobs.

Chapter Thirteen:
Student Congress

Controversial Newspaper Article Exercise

This section is where my course begins. I have students do a homework assignment to find a current issue in a newspaper article and to explain why it is controversial. Before you start, you need to understand that *controversial* means the article must have two opposing sides. The next day, you present your article in front of the class. The important understanding here is that the article needs to be controversial.

What Needs to be Changed in Society?

The format of the following information on student congress comes from the 2001 Student Congress Manual published by the National Forensic League (Student Congress Manual).

To begin, the instructor asks the class, "What needs to be changed in society?" Sometimes the students' answers may be something like the current curfew. The instructor would then ask, "What about the curfew needs to be changed?" The students may respond that it needs to be eliminated. Now we have a good start to a resolution. The instructor writes on the board:

Rules	Sample Resolution
1. All resolutions need a title. 2. All resolutions need "whereas" clauses that serve as reasons. 3. All "whereas" clauses need to be numbered. The reason is to insure clarity when students speak about and debate the legislation. 4. The "be it resolved" clause restates the purpose of the resolution.	A Resolution Concerning the Elimination of Curfew Laws 1. Whereas, the current curfew laws 2. discriminate against teens in our 3. community. 4. Whereas, some teenagers are forced 5. to violate curfew laws because they must 6. work beyond the designated time. 7. Whereas, parents should be the ones 8. to say when their children should have 9. to return home. 10. Whereas, many worthwhile youth 11. activities take place at night and run the 12. risk of violating curfew, making those 13. participants criminals. 14. BE IT RESOLVED by the student 15. congress assembled that the curfew 16. law should be eliminated. (Student name signed) (Student name typed)

Now you know how to write a simple resolution. By virtue of the fact that you have been researching news because of the Controversial Newspaper Article Exercise, you should come up with good topics.

Your selected topic needs to be approved by the instructor. Remember, you will want to do a resolution on a unique issue, so it's first-come first-serve on topics. Some recent topics that may work well are: driving age requirements, gun control, prayer in school, gay marriages, capital punishment, DUI law enforcement, speeding laws, lowering the voting age, minors should not pay taxes, minors should be treated as adults for serious crimes, improve urban transportation, improve homeless shelters, eliminate parking meters, create more skate parks, school start times, make education compulsory to the age of eighteen, eliminate the electoral college, ban tobacco, end curfew laws, end congressional filibustering, mandatory uniforms in schools, a resolution forcing banks to pay back bailout money before loaning money to other large banks, etc.

You will need to do research in a library with computers handy to create your resolutions. Resolutions can also be typed at home, depending on the school setting. On pages 132 and 133 are two sheets that will help you with your speech. The Congress Speech Rubric and Scoring Guide is a sample that will help you know what guidelines to follow. The Congress Speech Worksheet will help you organize your speech.

With a compilation of the entire class's resolutions in hand, you go to the library to research others' resolutions.

Now it is time for you to begin the congress. You each will create name cards so that your last names are visible to the front of the class. Pay particular attention to the following dialogue as this is how your congress will run.

The presiding officer (PO) is the person who runs the congress. The Secretary assists the PO in keeping good records.

Beginning of Congress

PO: This congress is now in session. Secretary, please read the title of resolution A. (Secretary reads the title.) Is there an authorship speech? Representative (Insert last name of author here. The Representative gives the speech.). Are there any questions? (Usually I allow three questions maximum to insure that there is more time for speeches than questions.) Yes, Representative (Insert last name of Rep asking question.)

Rep: Would the speaker please yield to a question?

After Questions

PO: Thank you, Representative (Insert last name). Seeing as that was an authorship speech, is there an opponent speech? (PO selects speaker.)

After proponent speech and questions

PO: Thank you, Representative (Insert last name). Seeing as that was an opponent speech, is there a proponent speech?

Repeat same method as before until there are no more speeches on the legislation.

In the basic public speaking class, we don't deal with sophisticated motions, we just vote after all the speeches have been given on a particular resolution. The concept of precedence is taught as the one who has spoken most recently loses his or her chance to speak when more than one hand is raised to give the same opponent/proponent speech.

Attention-Getting Device: Creating Congress Speeches

The *attention-getting device,* or AGD, is the way to introduce a topic by getting the audience interested in the speech and the content. This tactic works well for all public speaking occasions. Some types of AGD are the daunting statistic, the famous quotation, and the interesting scenario.

A *daunting statistic* is a great way to introduce a speech. For example, if one were to start a speech on AIDS in Africa by stating that over twenty-five million people there have AIDS, that statistic would definitely capture the audience. One way to color a statistic is to compare it to something the audience is more familiar with. For instance, if we take the same twenty-five million figure and compare it by saying that is more than the entire population of New York City and Los Angeles combined, the audience will have a reference as to how many people that figure represents.

A *great quotation* needs to be researched. You can find them in famous quotation books or online. Usually a quotation begins with the actual quote first, and then color it by citing the famous person who said it. Another viable strategy you can use is to begin the quotation by stating the situation surrounding the person who said

59

it. For example, "As Benjamin Franklin was leaving Independence Hall in Philadelphia after spending many hours devising the U.S. Constitution, he came to the crowded square when an elderly lady approached him and asked, 'What have you given us?' to which he replied, 'A democracy, ma'am, if you can keep it.'" In his book *Lend Me Your Ears: Great Speeches in History,* William Saffire reminisces about how President Richard Nixon gathered his writers together and said, "Never give me a naked quote. Put a little story in it" (22).

While the quotation and statistic work well to introduce an issue to the audience, the *interesting scenario* is a good way to develop an AGD with very little time.

You can use this type of AGD to put the listener into the place of someone directly affected by the resolution. One example could be: "Imagine a child with no place to go after school, except out on the streets of a violent neighborhood. The law of the street is the same as the law of survival. If we agree to pass this resolution for the implementation of after school programs, then that child would have better chances to succeed in a friendlier, less hostile environment. Now imagine that that child is you, or someone you love. Wouldn't you want to give yourself or that loved one a chance to succeed?" The scenario works well to connect not only to the audience, but also to the potential impact of the resolution.

Section Three:
THE COMPETITIVE
PUBLIC SPEAKING
EVENTS

Chapter Fourteen:
Introduction to the Competitive Public Speaking Events

If you are excited about competing in public speaking tournaments, these events are for you! Make no mistake, you need to be dedicated to the speech program. This section will give an overview of Original Oratory, Extemporaneous Speaking, Cross-Examination, and Lincoln-Douglas Debate. The Public Forum event is also a competitive event, but was explained in Chapter Seven: Basic Debate.

The Original Oratory is an eight- to ten-minute oration designed to entertain the audience while making them aware of a universal problem that needs to be corrected. This event takes several teacher/student conferences to prepare you to memorize a speech. In this section, there will be examples from three national finalist oratories from the 2002 Nationals held in Charlotte, North Carolina.

Extemporaneous Speaking requires you to prepare a variety of speeches on current events. The students need to practice both to polish speaking skills and to become familiar with history and current events of the world.

If you are interested in debate, Cross-Examination is considered the most challenging event. This event requires a team of two to compete. You will develop cases on one topic of national concern throughout the year. Many students attend debate camps around the country to prepare for their upcoming year of competition. This event is considered by many to be the most prestigious.

Finally, Lincoln-Douglas, or Value Debate, finishes the public speaking side of the competitive events. You may like this one-on-one type of debate. Students work from the context of which value is superior. Often, the bimonthly topics reflect the conflict surrounding security versus liberty.

Chapter Fifteen:
Original Oratory

Your purpose in creating an Original Oratory is to introduce the audience to a problem and to persuade the listeners as to a course of action or thought. Through a variety of attention-getting techniques (for more on attention-getting techniques, see page 59), you point out the origins of the problem along with the impacts that an issue has on everyone within society. The fact that the problem must be exposed as universal is crucial to establishing a pertinent topic. It is important to consider universal appeal. The orator presents the issue in a sense that the audience can see the existence and the importance of the issue. Finally, in this section you will read about analysis of the Original Oratory finalists along with their abilities to use stylistic devices common to the event.

The Original Oratory should open with an attention-getting device. One attention-getting device includes the use of humor. Another attention-getter could be the surprise factor. For example, one student used the surprise factor by rattling off reasons why not to speak. Although this tactic sometimes works — as it evidently had for him because he got to a final round of six out of 196 qualifiers nationwide — the student in the example above failed to establish a mood. The audience could see no connection to his introduction and the rest of his speech, entitled "A Whole Cool World." The body of his speech continued to demonstrate what it means to be hip. Unfortunately, his attempt at an attention-getter made the rest of his speech appear disjointed. If he had waited to get the attention of the audience before he started, perhaps his intent could have been more easily recognized. An example of a successful attention-getter would be another finalist's speech entitled, "The Duh Birds." She tells the story of the Dutch discovering a bird in the East Indies that had the odd quirk of running straight to its predator. Thus, the discovery of the quickly extinct Dodo bird.

In addition to the stylistic attention-getting device, there needs to be a coherent and original form of organization. A word used to express verbal outlining is *signposting* or *road mapping*. These terms mean to label the points consistently throughout the speech. This technique can be delivered as simply as stating point a, b, c, and so on. Another way to deliver the form of signposting, and especially important to Original Oratory, is to have a template where the organization follows a recognizable pattern. One student in the 2002 final wrote about what it takes to complete a life in her speech entitled "The Fourth String." She compares important life elements to the four strings on a violin and uses the example of a concert violinist who performs a concert with one string broken. The strings of the violin become a metaphor for a worthwhile life. As the previous example indicates, there are many ways to create a template through internal signposting. The reason for using signposting in an Original Oratory is to give the audience a clear idea as to where the speech goes.

Brent C. Oberg, a national finalist in oratory, explains the importance of organization in his book, *Speechcraft,* "Studies have shown that people who hear speeches that are structured are more likely to understand, remember, and be persuaded by the message compared to people who hear the exact same material without structure" (59). Cohesive structure not only helps audiences to remember points made, but also makes the speech easier to follow.

Sometimes organization comes in the form of verbal outlining or signposting. Yet, there are a variety of ways to make the flow of the oration seamless. One technique you could use is to compare a universal problem, such as verbal abuse, to a multi-course meal. Here you could start out, "If we were to compare the phenomenon of verbal abuse to a five-course meal at a restaurant, our appetizer might resemble an innocuous insult." You might save the main course for racial slurs, with the sexual innuendo reserved for dessert. You would then go on to illustrate the specifics with research.

You should consider using the following literary techniques in the creation of your speeches:

1. Parallel structure places two separate elements as equals. John F. Kennedy once said, "If a free society cannot help the many who are poor, it cannot save the few who are rich."

2. Tripartite division breaks a statement down into three parts. For example, Abraham Lincoln said, "We cannot dedicate, we cannot consecrate, we cannot hallow this ground."

Franklin Delano Roosevelt said, "I see one-third of a nation ill-housed, ill-clad, ill-nourished." A football coach might say, "We will attack, we will hit hard, we will execute."

3. Imagery is the literary device that allows the reader to see a vivid picture that the author creates.

4. Simile and metaphor are the comparison of unlike objects.

5. Hyperbole draws attention through overstatement.

6. Understatement presents something less than what it really is. To say, "Pele was an OK football player" is an example of understatement.

7. Alliteration is the use of repeated consonant sounds.

Literary techniques are just a few of the figures of speech used to enhance an Original Oratory. Sometimes you may start an Original Oratory with the idea that you will use at least four instances of parallelism, three examples of alliteration, and so on. This strategy will help you to develop conventions in speech writing. Also, it will make your speeches easy to listen to.

Another aspect of the Original Oratory is statistics. How should you deal with statistics? Statistics are important to establish credibility. For a concrete illustration of how to use numbers, turn back to chapter thirteen and see *daunting statistics* under the subhead Attention-Getting Device: Creating Congress Speeches on page 59. In addition, in his book *Forensics: The Winner's Guide to Speech Contests,* Brent Oberg explains three ways to make numbers memorable:

1. Make the statistics seem real to your audience. Explain how many of them may die as the result of a traffic accident.

2. Put statistics in simple terms. Do not state, "nine hundred, eighty-five thousand, nine hundred and ninety-two." Instead, state, "Just under a million." Reduce statistics to their simplest terms. "One out of every four Americans" sounds much better than the numeric counterpart.

3. Be graphic. Paint a picture with numbers. When James R. Fullam, Vice President of Sperry, illustrated the construction of the Epcot Center, he said "The construction work required moving fifty-four million cubic feet of earth to fill what was once a swamp. That meant moving enough earth to fill the New Orleans Superdome" (40-41).

You, as the writer, become an effective orator using these methods of delivering statistics.

To help you prepare an Original Oratory, use the Oratory Prep Sheet on page 134 as a guide.

Exercises and Activities for the Original Oratory

Original Oratory activities require you to extend your imagination. One of the most difficult parts of an Original Oratory is to come up with a topic. There are a couple of different ways to do so. One method is for you to write down two or three of the most intriguing ideas you have heard and explain why these may work. You should explore as much of the ideas as you possibly can. Write at least one page on an interesting topic. Look at the following examples and explain the components of what makes a good topic.

1. A good topic needs to have universal appeal. A personal story fails to encompass the far-reaching implications of universal appeal in most cases. In other words, a student should not predicate his or her Original Oratory on the need to increase school funding on extracurricular activities simply because the band program at the school suffered severe cuts and now that student is relegated to join the speech team in lieu of the preferred band activity.

2. A good topic needs to be original. Many topics become cliché and maybe fit the universal appeal, but are overdone and lose that spark of creativity that keeps an audience interested.

3. A good topic is provocative and leads one to consider a variety of possibilities. The audience can easily follow the main idea and get a feel for the importance of the presentation when the topic is introduced.

After reading and discussing these ideas, try and come up with topics that appeal to you. Write out your ideas. When considering an idea, ask yourself the following questions: How does the topic have universal appeal? How is my idea original, or, how can my idea be original? How is the topic provocative?

You can participate in a round-table discussion on an important topic with your mates in addition to or in place of the previous activity. A current issue that most students discuss is the invasion of Iraq and American use of torture and extraordinary rendition of al-Queda suspects. A topic might focus more on working with others to achieve a common goal than for one man to recklessly send an army to needlessly destroy others. Conversely, a topic from the same issue could emerge as the necessity of one strong individual to protect the world. Or, students could argue the importance of forbearance versus that of the necessity to act. Either of which could be developed into an Original Oratory somehow connected to the U.S. invasion of Iraq or use of torture.

Another effective technique in developing an Original Oratory is the use of language. You should work language and literary devices into your speeches as a way to develop an Original Oratory. You can practice funny stories that illustrate a point. Write phrases using alliteration, assonance, metaphor, simile, and the other literary terms explained previously in the chapter. See how many of these techniques you can include in a page or paragraph.

One excellent activity for developing the body of the speech is to go on a library scavenger hunt. Here you can find a variety of sources from novels and books to magazines and newspapers. You can incorporate a diversity of sources during this activity. These activities all take time to pursue. The time varies depending on you and your idea.

Chapter Sixteen:
Extemporaneous Speaking

Extemporaneous Speaking opens the door to a depth and breadth of knowledge. In this event you learn to research current events, their causes, significance, and the possible outcomes of various solutions. An individual participating in this event may deliver hundreds of speeches at national and world events over the course of a speech season. The way to learn Extemporaneous Speaking is to break down the speechwriting process. That process has four basic parts:

1. The attention-getting device
2. The preview of points
3. The body of the speech
4. The conclusion of the speech

As the writer, you use these elements to persuade the audience about a current national or world issue within the guidelines set by the National Forensic League.

At the beginning of each round, you receive three questions on domestic or foreign topics. You will select one and prepare a seven-minute speech in a thirty-minute preparation period. At the national level, a speaker will incorporate a large number of sources, statistics, and pertinent names from current magazines and books. Continuity is essential in organizing an Extemporaneous Speech. In other words, both the original orator and the extemporaneous speaker capture the audience and organize their talks. As with the original orator, the extemporaneous speaker needs to organize the speech so that the audience can follow it.

You can introduce your speech with a clever joke, anecdote, or quip. The attention-getting device is critical to setting up the speech. In his book *The Enlightened Storyteller*, Elijah Yip explains your obligations in a good attention-getter: "It is the extemper's responsibility to pique the interest of the audience so that he or she may establish a good rapport with them. Consequently, the first element of an introduction is the attention-getting device" (31). The attention-getting device serves to bring the audience into the speech. A good beginning is the first ingredient to a great extemporaneous speech. For more on attention-getting devices, see page 59.

After the attention-getting device, you state the extemporaneous question verbatim, preview the points, and work to set up the body of the speech. The extemporaneous speaker uses a verbal outline, or signposting, to let the audience know what to expect. The writer creates a brief preview, commonly referred to as a road map. A good road map consists of labels for each main point. Make sure the labels are in parallel form. In other words, they share an analytical progression or ingratiating thematic consistency. The labels are easy to remember and sufficiently informative at the same time to design creative labels. An example of a current preview or road map would be, "There are three reasons for the U. S. to significantly increase its foreign aid budget. Number one: having a positive presence in more areas of the world could mitigate the escalating cost of defense. Number two: increasing foreign aid could help poorer countries develop, thereby creating markets for U. S. producers. Number three: with rising poverty in Southeast Asia and Africa, coupled with the continuing AIDS epidemic, there is a need for U. S. assistance." Once you achieve a clear preview of points, you need to move on to the next step of the speech.

This portion of the speech is called the body. The body fills the bulk of speech time. Its purpose is to answer the topic question as fully and with as much depth as a seven-minute time limit allows. If the topic question asks, "What should" or "How can," the body will describe and evaluate course and cures to the problem noted. If the topic asks "Can" or "Should," the body will say "yes" or "no" with numerous evidenced reasons why you take that position.

You should use a wide array of periodicals, books, and news programs. In fact, the diversity of sources is a good indicator that you are widely read on the topic at hand. The sources include newspapers, think tanks, and magazines such as *The Economist, The Cato Institute, Foreign Affairs, Business Week, The Rolling Stone, The Christian Science Monitor, Le Monde Diplomatique* and *The New York Times,* just to name a few. Finalists at nationals in the extemporaneous categories used an average of seven different sources. You will keep articles in a file box where you maintain highlighted files on current events. Competitors maintain research by constantly clipping out new articles and placing them under a variety of headings.

Once you have your information, you need to examine the organization of your speech. A logical organizational pattern helps the judges to comprehend all of the information that is thrown at them during the course of the speech. A good speech is easy to understand because it is structured in a way that fosters the audience's reception, comprehension, and agreement with the speaker's message. In other words, good organization enhances persuasion.

In an edition of the *Rostrum* magazine, William Bennett examines the most common strategies for organizing an extemporaneous speech.

1. Topical Order is the most commonly used pattern or organization. The topic is broken down into "sub-topics," which are smaller divisions of the main topic. For instance, George Grimes and L.D. Naeglin note that the question, "How should Congress balance the federal budget?" could be examined in the sub-points tax increases, social service cuts, and defense cuts.

2. Criteria-Evaluation Order is a pattern for organization that establishes criteria for understanding the topic in one point and then analyzes the problem according to the criteria in the next point. For instance, if you were asked the chances of a certain presidential candidate, you could establish criteria for a viable presidential candidate — leadership qualities, experience, national popularity — and then evaluate how well the candidate in question meets your criteria.

3. Chronological Order divides your speech into time units, usually from the past, to present, to future to discuss the effect of a certain event. If looking at the question, "What effect did the terrorist attacks of 9/11 have on the U.S. Military?" one could analyze the military before the attacks, during the campaign against the Taliban, the subsequent war in Iraq, and the prospects for the future.

4. Space Order is organization that looks at an issue by region or area. If you were asked the effect of a certain policy or piece of legislation upon America, you could examine its effect in the eastern states, the Midwest, and in the West.

5. Two-sided Order is a form that takes both sides of a controversial issue. The speaker examines the main arguments for one side of an issue. Then the opposing arguments are examined. The speaker concludes that given the information, one side is preferable to the other.

6. Problem-Solution Order is a pattern of organization where you show that a serious problem has arisen, the significance and impact of that problem to individuals, and then suggest a way the problem may be solved. If you were asked the effect of rising tuition costs at American colleges and universities, you could show that tuition is rising at a dramatic pace, is a problem as it denies certain individuals a college education, and then point out how price controls at certain universities have been an effective means of solving this problem (24).

You should remain consistent with the chosen strategy. Seldom do these forms of organization intermingle well. Once the attention-getter, the preview, and the body are delivered, you conclude the speech.

In Brent Oberg's *Forensics: The Winner's Guide to Speech Contests*, he describes three goals of the conclusion:

1. Show how the speaker answers the question.
2. Summarize the main points.
3. Tie back to the opening of the speech (81).

What he means by the first rule is that you need to reinforce the stated answer to the question. There should be no doubt left as what the answer is and why. The second point means that you should review the body of the speech to include all the important information. You tie your speech together with the third point by bringing the audience back to the attention-getter.

Extemporaneous Speaking contains several elements. The environment helps you understand what you will go through during a competition. The attention-getter allows you to recognize the importance of captivating an audience from the beginning of the speech. With a preview of points, you guide the speech, allowing the audience to anticipate the direction and content. Through the body, you deliver the foundation of the presentation. Finally, the conclusion is thorough in reviewing the main points and the answer to the question.

On pages 135 to 137 are three easy-to-use guides of how to organize a speech: Extemporaneous Prep Sheet, Extemporaneous Prep Sheet Pro/Con Format, and Extemporaneous Prep Sheet Problem/Solution.

Exercises and Activities for Extemporaneous Speaking

After you have researched your extemporaneous topics, try to guess and brainstorm questions implied in your research. It should take about twenty minutes or so to write down the questions you find. After you and your mates come up with several topics each, you can share your ideas. Then select a topic you can speak on. At first, you should treat the practice more like a short impromptu than a full-blown extemporaneous speech. In other words, read the articles and draft a short speech in about ten minutes, including your speaking time. This practice gets you into the habit of thinking on your feet. Even seasoned competitors benefit from this repetition.

Another activity is researching the attention-getting device through anecdotes, quips, parables, quotations, and scenarios. A good way to practice this is for you to develop a previously given impromptu with the added faction of creating a good attention-getting device. Get a book on Aesop's fables or quotations by Will Rogers to act as a guide. Sometimes visual descriptions of political cartoons work well with the attention-getting device. Moreover, you can vary this type of practice by introducing a topic through an attention-getter.

Other activities include word choice orientation where you learn to select words carefully. Look at the chapter on transitions and verb activation on page 43. Look at the list of transitions in that chapter and use at least three of these within your speech. Similarly, use the verb activation list containing active verbs and eliminate some of the smaller helping verbs. Here, try to use at least three of the verbs on the sheet in your short speech.

In addition to the importance of content and word choice is your visual presentation style. A useful tool to help is video equipment. Once you see how you present, you can see how to improve the speech.

Your movement is essential in extemporaneous or oratory and video can be a valuable tool. Sometimes, to show you the effectiveness of your movement, you don't need to review the tape at normal speed. Fast forward the tape and you can see if your movement is stiff or choppy. Also, the video can assist you with issues concerning unnecessary phrase repetition.

Finally, once you are ready to compete, a rehearsal activity is to have three topics randomly selected from a larger pool, and you research from the evidence box on one topic for thirty minutes, and then give a full-blown extemporaneous speech. During the speech, the instructor writes comments, either on an extemporaneous speaking ballot, or just a simple piece of paper. After the presentation, the instructor and the student confer and rehash the speech.

Chapter Seventeen:
Cross-Examination

There are two main forms of competitive debate in high school. One is Cross-Examination, or Policy Debate, and the other is Lincoln-Douglas, or Value Debate. The primary difference between the two is that Lincoln-Douglas centers on comparing and contrasting philosophical values, whereas Cross-Examination focuses on changing policy. Values are socially accepted principles upon which we live. Policy, on the other hand, seeks to change current law to create new policy or change existing policy.

If you choose to try Cross-Examination, or Policy Debate, be prepared to spend in the neighborhood of twenty or so hours with your coach developing your case. Cross-Examination debate is where you debate the merits of changing current U. S. policy toward any issue. There are two students to a side — two on each team. The topic is selected each year via a nationwide vote among debate coaches. The affirmative case should assemble a position, or *white* paper, seeking to change a current U. S. policy. A white paper is what presidential advisors draft at the request of the president to recommend a course of action on a certain situation.

While the affirmative side seeks to explain why the U.S. should change policy, the negative counters that either the current policy works or the affirmative plan is flawed. For many judges the negative needs to refute only one of the key stock issues in order to win the debate. Therefore, the execution of the stock issues becomes the affirmative burden throughout the debate. The most common stock issues are: topicality, harms, inherency, significance, and solvency. Some coaches and judges expand the list to include disadvantages, counter plans, and justification. Remember, to debate this issue, you need to be able to work both sides, the negative and the affirmative side of the selected topic.

Topicality: This stock issue tests the affirmative staying to the topic. The case clearly falls under the resolution by having the government create an agency or other organization.

Harms: The current problem must create some harm to society. The affirmative presents statistics as evidence. Facts should be cross-referenced with credible, recent sources to prove the existence of a major problem.

Inherency: This stock issue explains what we are doing to allow the harm to exist. Additionally, an inherent barrier could explain the reasons why society overlooks the problem.

Significance: Significance begs the question, "Is the problem important enough to take the time and energy of policy makers?" Do the harms involved present a significant threat to domestic tranquility? The other aspect of this stock issue concerns the affirmative plan of attack. Will the plan significantly reduce the threat posed by the problem?

Solvency: Solvency is part of the affirmative plan of action. Will the proposal, or plan presented in the case, solve the problem presented in the harms? A proposal or plan of action needs to include any means necessary to solve the problem. A workable plan includes advantages. What are the advantages and chances of success behind the implementation of the program?

Of the five stock issues mentioned above, inherency and plan require more detailed explanation. The first affirmative constructive speech needs to incorporate topicality, harms, inherency, and significance in an eight-minute speech. The plan includes solvency and some aspects of significance. The plan may be presented in the second affirmative constructive speech, but can also be explained in the first affirmative speech — also called the 1AC. The negative needs to prove that one of the stock issues is not workable in order to win the debate round. A *round* is one debate.

The most intriguing and misunderstood stock issue is inherency. In other words, your most difficult argument to prove is the one postulating that the status quo, or what is happening now, maintains the problem requiring the resolution.

Once the affirmative establishes harms and significance, showing that the issue is worthy of the time and energy of policy makers, inherency comes into play when harms are built into the present system. Thus, the problem is inherent. Inherency requires the investigator to locate the causes of the problem and show they cannot be eliminated by anything short of policy change. In completing this aspect, the case establishes a unique rationale for the adoption of the policy. If the harms go away without intervention, then there is no reason to change policy. Therefore, the negative may argue that the present system recognizes the problem and has policy in place to reduce the currents harms. In order to establish and combat inherency, it is important to preview this section on inherent barriers. The following ways demonstrate inherent barriers preventing the resolution: gaps in the present system, a set of barriers, private sector issues, and current policy. The affirmative selects any one or combination of these to bolster the inherency argument.

Your first way to establish inherency identifies gaps in the laws and programs of the present system. Often, problems arise that the current system did not anticipate. An example can be found in the civil rights arguments. The U. S. Constitution originally guaranteed rights to American citizens, but did not specifically include voting rights for American women and African Americans. Otherwise stated, there was a gap in the present system regarding the protecting of civil rights. In the twentieth century, as Americans gradually came to see women and African Americans as deprived citizens, these gaps became noticeable and the system had to be changed.

Another way to establish inherency illustrates that the present policy contains a set of barriers to the elimination of the harm. Returning to the civil rights issue, even though women and African Americans received the right to vote in the early twentieth century, the manner of voting was left up to each state. The rules varied from state to state and were discriminatory in that they forced poll taxes on the impoverished and literacy tests for the uneducated. Unfortunately, the status quo rules of state-run elections constituted a barrier to participation in government, even though the system apparently filled in the gap by constitutional change. If the government chooses an inappropriate method to enact its own commitments, that method creates a barrier to successful change.

The negative might counter that the government method needs more time and, therefore, is not the problem. The evidence presented makes the difference between the arguments. If one side *postdates* — the evidence is newer — the other, that may win the argument.

Inherency arguments can also focus on the private sector rather than on the government. To continue with the civil rights example, the real problem of inequality exists not entirely with government actions. The concern also stems from unchecked racism brought on by the private sector. Not only was it standard not to pay white women and African Americans a wage, making employment itself a policy of discrimination, society relied primarily on white-owned businesses. Therefore, social attitudes of the time prevailed upon society to promote prejudice. Now, the negative may counter that, despite the racism, the government does not have the obligation to interfere in the private sector over issues concerning prevailing moral sentiment. The example presented, however, may be difficult for the negative to refute.

Other manifestations of inherency center on the implementation of current government policies. Because government policies can be the product of compromise, different administrations emphasize some programs more than others. Therefore, a successful inherency argument could call for the elimination of government activity in a special policy area. For example, if the topic called for a comprehensive farms policy, a good inherency argument for the affirmative would be to deregulate farm prices. You would state that the free market provides a more efficient system of supply than the government subsidy program. In this example, you prove the government interference in the marketplace causes the farming problem. Another example could be an argument for the elimination of phone taps on private lines, arguing that such activity needlessly intrudes on personal liberties. The inherency in this case is the discretionary power of the government to use any means of surveillance available. Never is this more relevant than today, where the Obama Administration is faced with coming to grips with liberty versus security as a product of the Patriot Act. Therefore, the case-by-case decision-making on wiretapping is too uncertain to guarantee rights. However, the negative may refute this argument by mentioning the security of the nation as a whole is at risk without wiretaps, especially considering the current War on Terror.

Once harms, significance, and inherency surface to prove the necessity of the resolution, the affirmative postulates a plan designed to eliminate harms and inherent barriers. Now the last of the stock issues, solvency, arises. Does the plan solve the harms? Mandates make up the plan. Certain mandates may include, but are not limited to: funding, enforcement, agency or policy development.

You could establish your plan in *planks,* to organize the plan, which contains funding, enforcement, and delivery. One way to acquire the necessary funds to implement a plan is to raise taxes. Another method used to create means for a plan could be to divert existing responsibilities of current agencies to act toward the problem at hand. The negative could state that the public will not stand for additional taxes, despite what the benefits of such government revenue could be.

Enforcement becomes the next step toward implementing a plan. Once a viable plan is in place, you need to ask yourself, "How does enforcement work to maintain it?" Your type of enforcement depends on your plan to solve the problem and promote the resolution. Enforcement could be to establish an agency to monitor the enactment of the plan. The negative often argues that enforcement may not be workable in the face of such sweeping changes.

Another area to be considered on the plan side of the debate is the creation of a new agency or branch within an existing agency, designed to solve the problem at hand. This plank becomes another governmental branch, or another task within an existing branch, serving to eliminate the harms caused by the problems resulting in the necessity of the resolution. One problem with the creation of a new agency is the difficulty in proving the possible effectiveness of a nonexistent branch of the government. The negative team may suggest that there already is a branch working to solve the harms brought out in the first affirmative speech.

A final result of establishing solvency in the debate becomes the advantages as illustrated in the plan. Your advantages could result in the elimination of a certain threat or the improvement of U.S. foreign policy depending on the topic. As negative you could refute the advantages by mentioning the disadvantages noted by changing the status quo. Remember, these are disadvantages specific to the *plan,* not the harms. In fact, these disadvantages may be unintended results of the plan. Intensive evidence determines the quality of the arguments and presentation skills also reflect the art of persuasion.

The Overall Times of a Cross-Examination Debate

Eight minutes – first affirmative constructive speech

Three minutes – cross-examination

Eight minutes – first negative constructive speech

Three minutes – cross-examination

Eight minutes – second affirmative constructive speech

Three minutes – cross-examination

Eight minutes – second negative constructive speech

Five minutes – first negative rebuttal (No new arguments allowed in rebuttals. New evidence extends previous arguments.)

Five minutes — first affirmative rebuttal

Five minutes second – negative rebuttal

Five minutes second – affirmative rebuttal

Five minutes of preparation time allotted to each side to organize their cases during the debate

Exercises and Activities for Cross-Examination Debate

Activities for Cross-Examination Debate consist of delving into the library to find a variety of recent research and developing that information into something that bolsters a need for policy change. The prerequisite for a good case is many hours online and in the library getting information from scholarly research papers to a variety of expert opinions. There are several links on nflonline.org prompting students to debate camps and sites where they may find case ideas.

One way to practice listening skills in the policy format is for you to present an eight-minute constructive speech and have a mate create a one-minute highlight of that eight-minute speech by listening and reciting the main points delivered. During this summary, the summarizing student states the points in order of importance. Another benefit to this assignment could be for your listening partner to learn the use of prep time. You give your speech and afterward your partner gets about ninety seconds to prepare the summary.

Another good activity to practice a team's case is to work on cross-examination. Your team can work against another to simulate real round situations.

Finally, one way to continually develop new activities for practice sessions is to divide the events into segments and work one segment at a time. Here you work on elements of public speaking that are universally present in all areas. One area that pervades all of the public speaking events is presence and fluency. The command that you have on word choice and tempo indicates the confidence of a winner. The ability for you to plan and work on hand gestures and body position is a trained skill that needs development. Often gestures become too repetitive and do not enhance the flow of a speech. Many times policy debate consists merely of reading a brief a few inches away from the speaker's face at a rate of 400 words per minute. To move away from this style and to a more elegant speaking arrangement would make for a better speech. You can work on activities designed to help your presentation style.

Chapter Eighteen:
Lincoln-Douglas Debate

Imagine reliving the great debates between Stephen Douglas and Abraham Lincoln back in the mid-nineteenth century. That is the origin of Lincoln-Douglas Debate, also known as the Value Debate. Those two had famous debates for the Illinois U.S. Senate seat before the American Civil War. They argued over topics of slavery and ownership rights over individuals. Currently, the Lincoln-Douglas Debate is a value debate where you seek to affirm or negate a resolution based on the superiority of your value over the opponent's value.

During the six-minute affirmative segment, the affirmative postulates the key value that upholds arguments supporting your side. You introduce your core value with criteria serving as pillars which support it. You detail your speech through the use of a philosopher whose theory agrees in principle with the importance of your selected value.

A thirty-second quote from the philosopher or an historic scenario could preface this affirmative. After the preface, the affirmative introduces his stance on the resolution by stating the resolution verbatim, along with key definitions. A great source for defining terms in a debate is *Black's Law Dictionary*. Once the topic and stance of the affirmative have been introduced, then the affirmative proceeds to analyze the relevance of the quotation or scenario connecting its importance to the value and criterion.

You utilize language consistently serving to clarify the flow of thought. This language usually reflects outline form. In Lincoln-Douglas Debate, no matter if you are negative or affirmative — again, as with Cross-Examination, you will argue both sides in different debate — you will need to have a core value and a criterion. The argument has a core value, which is supported by a criterion. The criterion is the vehicle through which the value exists. The criterion and value combination results in the affirmation or negation of the resolution.

On the affirmative side, the criterion of voting leads to the value of democracy resulting in affirming the resolution that individual liberty is more important that social security. Contentions reflect the practical examples in which the criterion and value work to affirm the resolution.

You can use any of the following examples to outline their contentions. Subpoints are the specific instances reflected in the contention.

1. Value/Criterion — may be an initial concept introduced by the philosopher, or an idea that links the position of the philosopher to the main value.

A.) First Contention
    i. Subpoint A
    ii. Subpoint B
B.) Second Contention

The First Contention in a tag line is to relay the headline of a contention. Just as the idea of a newspaper headline provides a general idea as to the remainder of the article, the tag line presents the main premise of the contention. The contention needs to connect directly to the value and criterion resulting in the affirmation or negation of the resolution.

The introduction of subpoints becomes key when trying to establish depth in the contention used. When you use examples from everyday life, it serves to make the value, the philosopher's point, and the criteria more substantial and relative. The points presented need to have clear links. Another good rule is to discuss how the contention supports the value and criterion resulting in the affirmation of the resolution. The tighter affirmative cases tend to have one or two contentions that keep the affirmative more direct.

After the affirmative speech defines the key terms and presents a main value with supporting criteria, the negative prepares questions taken from notes during the first affirmative.

The questioning period is three minutes in length. The purpose of any questioning period becomes the chance to clarify the previous speech. In fact, in the first two constructive speeches you end with the phrase, "I now stand open for questions and points of clarification."

The questioning period could also be used to set up the negative constructive speech, or the affirmative initial response, by using answers to support one value over another.

Your negative constructive speech is seven minutes in length and usually the first three to four minutes are used to develop a value the same as the affirmative constructive. In the remaining time, the debater attacks the affirmative case through establishing a value clash. The negative seeks to make his value superior to the affirmative based on the affirmative case and the cross-examination period.

Specifically, your negative speech starts with a brief overview, or roadmap, of what you will cover over the course of the next seven minutes. Then, the negative states that he opposes the resolution. Usually, a quotation or a historic event begins the argument. The quotation could be from a noted philosopher. As negative, you can then elaborate on the philosopher's meaning throughout the case. A successful case places the criterion that upholds the value resulting in the negation of the resolution.

The next portion of the debate is the three-minute cross-examination period where the affirmative seeks clarification to the negative's case and attacks. During the next phase, the affirmative has four minutes to respond to the negative's case and rebuild his or her own constructive. During this period, the affirmative answers the value attacks and extends his or her own value as superior in the debate round. The affirmative seeks to crystallize the negative arguments and refute them. This portion of the debate seeks an affirmative ballot.

The final negative speech follows and takes six minutes to answer attacks and wrap up the case by reiterating how the negative value remains intact despite the affirmative attacks. The negative carefully tracks each important argument in the debate to reaffirm the position. Although the negative can introduce new evidence to extend previous arguments, no new arguments are allowed in the rebuttal.

The final affirmative speech is a short, three-minute rebuttal. As with the negative rebuttal, the affirmative tracks, or crystallizes, the main arguments and proves his or her value as superior.

During the debate each side takes three minutes to prepare arguments.

The format is as follows:

Six Minutes — affirmative constructive

Three Minutes — negative cross-examination

Seven Minutes — negative constructive and attack

Three Minutes — affirmative cross-examination

Four Minutes — affirmative response (No new arguments allowed during rebuttal/ response period. New evidence extends previous arguments.)

Six minutes — negative rebuttal

Three minutes — affirmative rebuttal

Lincoln-Douglas Debates center on the discussion of a value to affirm or negate a resolution. The topic is selected bimonthly, but basically comes down to the rights of the individual or smaller societies against those of the majority. A typical topic example used at the national tournament is "Resolved that laws to protect people from themselves are justified." This type of debate differs in content from Extemporaneous Speaking in that it does not require the content-specific details.

The final round at a National Forensic League Championship consisted of two debaters out of 202 qualifiers. The affirmative selects a value of justice supported by the criterion of rights protection. The negative, on the other hand, selects humanity as defined by human rationalism supported by the criterion of autonomy. In the affirmative case, there are four contentions. The first contention argues that people do not have requisite knowledge in all things to know what is best for them. The subpoint here is that the mentally or criminally ill do not possess the faculties to be held accountable for their actions. Therefore, paternalistic laws are necessary to keep them from making potentially dangerous decisions. Contention two postulates that since all people cannot be aware of the consequences of any given action, they therefore cannot be legally allowed to participate in a potentially dangerous activity. The subpoint here is John Stuart Mill's example of a dangerous bridge. If a bridge is damaged, then it should be illegal to use. The third contention is that of temporary or emotional unbalance. The subpoint is that those who want to commit suicide often want to live and need a holding period to allow them to make the right choice. The fourth contention is that outside factors have too much power over individuals, thereby necessitating paternal laws. One subpoint used here is that people might resort to dueling to settle disputes.

The negative constructive speech uses human rationality as a value supported by the criterion of autonomy. The first contention is that people have the authority over themselves resulting in the protection of human worth. The subpoint examples are: alcohol prohibition goes against certain religious practices and laws are too broad and must include all individuals. Thus, these paternal laws deny the worth of the individual. The second contention tag line is that paternal laws violate autonomy by hindering moral development. The reasoning here is that if adults are treated like children, they become children. Now, the above-mentioned time constraints of the negative's case limits scope of developing the case. Therefore, there were only two contentions delivered.

The negative attacks the affirmative position. The negative presents the core value clash that justice supported by rights protection does not work because it denies the people the opportunity to develop their own individual, autonomous rights. The government then undermines rights protection and therefore destroys autonomy. The attack against the affirmative first contention states that even if people do not have the capacity to know all situations, they still should have the autonomy to make their own decisions. Another attack against the affirmative first contention is that the majority of parents know what is best for their children without paternalistic laws. The attack against the affirmative's second contention states that education allows for the awareness of people to make considerate choices. The next attack against the affirmative's fourth contention mentions that while there are powerful external pressures on people, it does not make sense to concentrate all the power in the hands of the government.

The rebuttal speeches focus on three goals: rebuilding the case, extending attacks on the opponent's case and identifying for the judge voting issues, and how you are winning those issues. You learn to create on your feet. You deal with some advanced concepts in the supporting of your contentions.

The format and strategy of a Lincoln-Douglas Debate requires knowledge of how to organize through signposting, as with Original Oratory, Extemporaneous Speaking, and Cross-Examination. The ability to think while in a debate round is crucial to the formation of ideas.

You should continually connect the contention and the subpoint to the value and criterion throughout the case. Negative cases are shorter and do not require as much development. The contention establishes the physical existence of the value arising from the criterion leading to the negation or affirmation of the resolution. Cleverly constructed affirmative cases predict the opposing arguments and persuade against them before the negative has had a chance to speak.

For help organizing your debate, see page 138 for the Lincoln-Douglas Debate Worksheet.

Exercises and Activities for the Lincoln-Douglas Debate

There are several activities that can be done for Lincoln-Douglas Debate. You can look at a particular resolution and work to understand it. *Black's Law Dictionary* is the preferred source for that understanding. You can look up key terms in resolutions using this reference guide. Of course, any dictionary would be fine. If there are at least two students working on the same topic, one student develops a case for the affirmative and the other student develops the case for the negative, and they switch cases.

The hard part is getting to the case development. This takes time as you need to decide what values are at stake within a particular topic. One value fits one side and the other works in the opposing corner. You start by developing a small example proving the importance of your stated value.

Once you develop these values, you can practice by cross-examining each other. If the instructor is working with you, then he or she can write down questions and ask them during a practice cross-examination period. You learn to develop speeches and persuasive speaking styles through practice and research. You need to be aware of various philosophical principles espousing certain values.

One way to develop your understanding of philosophical ideas is for you and your mates to select a philosopher and write a quick two-page biography on that person. In the biography, come up with a value you think the philosopher would espouse and explain why. Although the Lincoln-Douglas Debate is not uniquely a debate over established philosophies, it is important to understand various schools of thought. The following are a few philosophers who you can select: Descartes, Espinoza, Locke, Rousseau, Kant, Nietzsche, Sartre, Hiedegger, Montesquieu, Einstien, Rawls, Justice Oliver Wendell Holmes, Plato, Socrates, Phaedrus, Marx, Adam Smith, Keynes, Pavlov, Einstein, Emerson, Thoreau, etc.

Section Four:
HONING YOUR SKILLS

Chapter Nineteen:
Readers Theatre

Readers theatre is a fantastic way for you to discover how to read and participate actively in course literature. Practically any novel or play can be set to a readers theatre format.

The activity explained below varies from the traditional setting where you sit on chairs and do readings. In this type of readers theatre, you act out roles and can invent situations that must have happened in books, but were only briefly alluded to. You build on your ability to infer and script-write.

The activity calls for you to reflect on the author's intent and to create an analysis that demonstrates not only your understanding of the material, but why we study literature. The discovery as to why literature is important can be fun when the class takes the journey of looking at a particular scene and comes up with unique interpretations.

To begin, the class divides into groups of five or six. Then you select a scene for your group to present. The classroom becomes a stage and your group brings in props to help with the interpretation of your scenes. You work together to bring their scene to life.

Here is a step-by-step guide to help you through the activity:

1. Organize your group and reflect on the piece you will develop.
2. Work out how you will present your scene.
3. Organize your roles — figure out who does what. Remember to work to individual strengths when devising roles. Students more comfortable with acting should take the lead acting position. Students better suited to analysis could narrate or work on the group's analysis. Divide roles and tasks evenly. No Slacking!
4. Brainstorm on the analysis. Think of ways to answer the following questions:
   a. How does your scene reflect the author's intent?
   b. How does your scene relate to the entire piece as a whole?

    c. How does your scene relate to modern-day situations? In other words, how is this scene important in today's world?

    d. The analysis can either come in the form of an introduction to begin the performance or a conclusion presented at the end of the selection. In any case, the group should have a brief statement at the beginning of the piece introducing the author, book, and scene so that the audience understands the basics of the scene before it is presented.

5. Scripts are not allowed, so feel free to make note cards to help with your scene. Rehearsing is key here. Use class time wisely.

6. The interpretation should be about one minute per group member. Therefore, if the group has five people, the minimum time is five minutes. If the group is six, then the minimum is six minutes. The introduction and analysis are included in the timing of the piece.

For more guidance, a sample rubric and a Readers Theatre Worksheet can be found on page 139.

Chapter Twenty:
Choral Reading

Here you are going to explore the interpretive side of public speaking. So far, this book has concentrated more on formal public speaking. The choral reading focus of the class gives you a glimpse in dramatic interpretation. In fact, Fran Tanner explains in her text *Creative Communication* that poetry is the material used in choral readings. She continues to state that sometimes this activity is called verse-speaking choir (262). Therefore, in addition to studying the art of interpretation, you will be studying poetry as well.

In addition to becoming familiar with some aspects of drama and poetry, you learn about stage direction and blocking. In this interpretive section, you learn to cheat out and look more toward the audience when participating in dialogue while you learn to use the space on the stage. You can create a stage in the classroom, or use the school theatre or lecture hall to give you a more thorough experience in the dramatic realm.

You can play with different accents in preparing your choral reading. For example, you can practice with a New York accent, or speak jive, or sound very, very old or very, very young. Can you, like, uh, do a valley girl impersonation? By practicing impersonations you already know, you will learn to color lines in a poem.

The following poems are examples that work well with choral reading:

"The Seven Ages of Man" by William Shakespeare

"The Charge of the Light Brigade" by Alfred Lord Tennyson

"The Jabberwocky" by Lewis Carroll

"I Hear America Singing" by Walt Whitman

"Eldorado" by Edgar A. Poe

"We Real Cool" by Gwendolyn Brooks

"Casey at the Bat" by Ernest Lawrence Thayer

"The Glove and the Lions" by Leigh Hunt

"The Sound of Silence" by Paul Simon

"The Highwayman" by Alfred Noyes

The Assignment

Students get into groups and select a poem they would like to perform as a choral selection. Each student or group-within-a-group of students reads a certain voice. You'll note that poems are made up of *voices,* or parts for the players to read. Each participant selects a voice or voices.

Once students select their voices, they think of a prop or costume to bring. Each player comes in costume. Be creative and original! The following is a diagram of the stage to help you with your blocking. A sample rubric can be found on page 140.

Upstage Right	Upstage Center	Upstage Left
Right	Center	Left
Downstage Right	Downstage Center	Downstage Left

(Audience)

Some Definitions You Need to Know

Blocking occurs after players choose their parts and do at least one read through. Blocking is the positioning and movement of each player on the stage. Typically, *footwork* puts the actor's body facing toward the crowd. This artificial positioning toward the crowd is called *cheating out.*

Chapter Twenty-One:

Negotiations

This chapter will take you through the life skill of negotiations. No one will argue the importance of negotiations as a public speaking and communicative skill. Studying negotiations in the classroom is both challenging and enlightening. You will understand the fact that you are already involved in negotiating on some level. Whether you have bargained the price of your first car, or how long your parents should let you stay out at night, chances are that most of you have participated in some form of negotiation.

The first strategy in learning this section is to ask yourself, "What is negotiation?" It should not take very long to come up with an operable definition of negotiations. After you understand a bit about the meaning of negotiations, brainstorm examples of negotiation tactics with your mates.

There are two activities in this section. The Negotiation Game is an interactive exercise used in the business world based on getting you to understand the importance of cooperation. The Negotiation Activity is a real world example of negotiation.

Terms to Know

Before the games begin, you should learn the following terms:

Caucus: where the group convenes in private to discuss making and accepting an offer

Anchor: a bona fide starting point in an offer

Counter offer: a compromise offer in response to an initial proposal

Walk away point: where one side is compelled to quit negotiations

Lead negotiator: in a negotiation between two sides, there should be a lead negotiator who can speak for the group to prevent the basic problem of too many people speaking at once

Negotiation Game

This game involves two sides, each with a lead negotiator making decisions that affect their side. In American culture, the natural reaction for us is to turn "cooperation" into "competition." There is a general reaction to try and get one side to do one thing in order to achieve an advantage.

Now, in order to understand this concept, you will play the game.

Step One: Divide up into two groups.

Step Two: Read the rules.

Step Three: Each group selects a lead negotiator. The group may change this person from round to round or keep the same person.

Step Four: Each group discusses the obvious strategy.

Step Five: When both groups are ready with their selections for round one, each lead negotiator meets in a secluded place and they discuss their cooperative strategy.

Step Six: The lead negotiators return to their respective groups and make a decision. In this scenario the groups decide on 1, 2, or 3.

Step Seven: The teacher writes the selection and the points on the board for each round. At the end of the last round, the points are tallied.

The Rules

The object of the game is for each team to get as many points as possible.

Both sides get three choices — the numbers 1, 2, or 3.

1. If team A selects 3 and team B selects 1, A receives A plus 2 team, B negative 2.

2. If team B selects 1 and Team A selects 2, then team B receives 2 points and A receives negative 2.

3. If team A selects 2 and team B selects 2, both teams receive 3 points.

4. If team A selects 2 and team B selects 3, team B receives 2 and team A receives positive 3.

5. If Team A selects 3 and team B selects 3, then team A receives 1 and team B receives 2.

6. If A selects 1 and B selects 3, B receives 2 and A receives negative 2.
7. If A selects 2 and B selects 3, A gets 2 and B receives negative 2.
8. If A selects 1 and B selects 2, A receives 2 B receives negative 2.
9. If A selects 3 and B selects 2, A receives negative 1 and B plus 1.
10. If A selects 2 and B selects 2, both receive a negative 2 points.

	Team A selection	Points	Team B Selection	Points
Round 1				
Round 2				
Round 3				
Round 4				
Round 5				
Round 6				
Round 7				
Round 8				
Round 9				
Total				

Negotiation Activity

The class divides into two groups. One is pro union and the other is pro company.

Each group must come up with a walk away point for their side and for the opposing side. The union has already listed their demands. The company team needs to caucus and discuss the union demands and come up with their counterproposal.

Read the following negotiation scenario and look at the proposal. Either you have drafted the proposal or you are deciding on accepting it, rejecting it, or making a counter offer. If you are on the company side, you can anticipate what you think the union will do and discuss the possibilities.

Union Side

The union workers at the Acme Food and Catering Services Corporation have not been given a raise in three years. They would like a standard of living increase that would amount to a total of 7% for the past three years and an additional 2% for the upcoming year. Currently, union members make $24,000 per year. A 7% increase would be $1,680. There are 500 employees who would need this compensation. Current benefits include two weeks paid vacation.

Company Side

The Acme Food and Catering Services Corporation has just landed a contract with Jones Construction, one of the largest union supporters in the country. The convention must be catered by union personnel. The leaders of Acme have $500,000 to negotiate with their union. It is vitally important for Acme Food and Catering Services Corporation to settle on the contract. The other benefits in play could be to add paid vacation days to the ten days the employees already receive.

Chapter Twenty-Two:
Trial in the Classroom

A trial is a great way for you to participate in an interactive lesson that demonstrates speaking and thinking skills while learning literature. The only criterion for a trial is that there should be a character who has done something illegal. There are two examples in this chapter that include parts for everyone in the class. Either you select the roles you want to play or the teacher chooses.

On page 140 is the Scoring Guide for the Salem Witch Trial sample rubric and on page 140 is the sample Rubric for the Trial of Henry Fleming for Desertion.

How It Works

Typically, the class will divide into two groups: prosecution and defense.

The *prosecution team* consists of a lawyer (prosecutor) or a few prosecutors who try the case. Also included in the prosecution team would be witnesses, usually characters from a given text who would be against the supposed wrongdoer.

The *defense team,* as in a real-life courtroom drama, consists of the lawyer representing the supposed wrongdoer. Witnesses can be called up who are sympathetic to the defense.

The jury writes a decision based on the evidence heard in court and read in the novel. There can be judges who understand the following about courtroom procedure:

Objections occur only when the line of questioning is out of order and doesn't serve the purpose of the court. They are only stated by the lawyer opposite the one doing the questioning. They only happen during a questioning period. *Overruled* means that the objection is not good and that the witness should answer the question. *Sustained* means that the objection is valid and that the questioning lawyer needs to rephrase his or her question or ask a different question.

The Format for the Trial

1. Opening remarks prosecution: A few minutes summarizing why the defendant committed the crime he or she is accused of.

2. Opening remarks defense: A few minutes stating why the defendant is innocent of the crime with which he or she is charged.

3. Prosecution makes its case: This is where the prosecution calls up witnesses, usually characters from the novel or play. Here students can use direct quotations or thoughts taken from the text for their questions and answers. The defense team may cross-examine each witness once the prosecution has completed initial questioning. After the presentation of all the witnesses, the prosecution rests.

4. The next phase of the trial is where the defense calls up its witnesses in much the same fashion as the prosecution. The prosecution can cross-examine the witnesses as the defense excuses them.

5. After the defense rests, the defense presents a closing statement where they state why the defendant is innocent of all charges and should be acquitted.

6. The prosecution then concludes the trial with closing arguments as to how during the trial the defendant is proved to be guilty.

In a legal courtroom, the prosecution always begins and finishes a trial. The reason for this advantage is because the prosecution has the disadvantage of burden of proof. For classroom purposes, though, this part can be switched for a more balanced trial.

For all of the above, the members of the jury and the judge are keeping notes and preparing a reason for decision — why the defendant is innocent or guilty.

Example One: The Salem Witch Trial

The Players

Witnesses for the Prosecution:	The Accused:
Hathorne	Giles Corey
Danforth	John Proctor
Hale	Francis Nurse
Parris	Mary Warren
Abigail	Elizabeth Proctor

Nurse   Martha Corey
Putnam   Rebecca Nurse
Mercy

The Assignment

The class is divided into five groups: the prosecution, the defense, the accused, witnesses for the prosecution, and judges.

First 15 minutes: The students research quotations that support the side they have chosen. Each student must create notes with at least two quotations and a brief summary as to how those quotations help their team.

Next 15 minutes: The witnesses for the prosecution present their case. Each character presents their side. A brief questioning period, conducted by the opposing side, follows each character's presentation.

Next 15 minutes: The defense presents their case. A brief questioning period follows each presenter.

Finale: The judges offer their written decision.

The Trial of Henry Fleming for Desertion

Prosecution: The objective of the prosecuting team is to prove Henry Fleming guilty of desertion and to seek the maximum penalty of death by firing squad.

Defense: The defense should ask for clemency from the jury. The defense needs to prove that although Henry did flee the battle scene, he had reasons that were patriotic. Be sure to discuss Henry's reasoning in his flight from the battle.

The Players:

Henry Fleming, the accused

The defense team

The prosecution

The judges' panel

The jury

Students need to first research those pages subsequent to Henry's flight from battle. Students discover quotations pertaining to Henry's feelings and thoughts going into battle. Also, Henry's rationale as to why he fled becomes a key issue in understanding the prosecution and defense. The judge and jury need to present objective arguments for both sides in anticipation of ensuing arguments.

Next, each participant prepares a written explanation of his or her position according to his or her role in the proceeding. The defense team uses specifics from the book to explain Henry's reasoning for deserting his post. The prosecution argues the facts, as found from the book, to promote the case. If there are two or more members in the prosecution, then each person presents his or her individual findings in addition to the other presentations. No overlapping! The judges' jury proposes a reason for a decision based on the accuracy of the facts presented. Each presentation is one page written.

Chapter Twenty-Three:
The Body Sculpture Activity

Variation One

The body sculpture activity is a great way for you to find thematic concepts within a piece of literature through the careful examination of a passage or phrase with a few of you acting out a freeze-frame that symbolically depicts that phrase and its greater meaning to the novel, play, or poem.

An entire class can come up with different body sculptures for one novel by participating in groups and selecting different passages that may reflect a common theme found throughout the novel. You can use props and put yourselves in a position that reflects a scene from a passage and the meaning of the entire novel, play, or poem.

Once the students from a group form a sculpture, the class looks at the sculpture and brainstorms the symbols presented and a theme. The instructor writes the brainstormed ideas on the board. Then the group sees if their sculpture got the intended point. In your preparation, be sure to write out a 500-word essay pointing out how you know that your interpretation reflects both the scene and the theme of the work. Scenes are selected on a first-come-first-serve basis.

For a sample Rubric for the Body Sculpture Activity, see page 140.

The Essay

The theme can be expressed in terms of the story and the passage. You explain how each position in your group portrait contributes to the theme. You can point out other aspects of your scene aside from positioning as part of the analysis.

Variation Two

The instructor assigns a passage and you get into pairs and try to create a small, two-person sculpture with a chair as a prop. Each pair presents their portrait and shares the meaning of their pose with the class.

Variation Three

The all-star body sculpture works from a group of commonly read selections during the course of a semester. Here you choose a well-known scene from several selections. This works like Variation One.

Chapter Twenty-Four:
The Found Poem and Found Story Assignments

The Found Poem

The Found Poem assignment is where you find a poem within a larger piece of work. In other words, you create a poem with lines taken from a novel or short story. This assignment works best when you select a topic for the poem. One positive outcome of the Found Poem is when you realize a theme as you research your poem from the text.

This assignment can be arranged in a variety of ways from a variety of texts. You are encouraged to find a story within a story. Often the story is a reflection of the larger piece from where you take your lines.

Short stories that have a dominant characteristic are ideal for this assignment. For example, Jack London's *To Build a Fire* sets a scene of a man battling the frigid temperatures of the Yukon. In this story, the reader is inundated with images of frozen snow in sixty below zero temperatures. A man struggles against the temperatures in a futile attempt to reach a camp. The cold becomes overwhelming as the man eventually freezes to death. The reason why this story is so good for the Found Poem assignment is because it has the constant plight of the man against the daunting cold of the Yukon.

Another story I use is a Frederick Douglas excerpt, "The Battle with Mr. Covey." This story is set in eighteenth century America where Douglas, a slave at the time, is rented out by his master to Mr. Covey who treats Douglas cruelly and they end up fighting. The reoccurring image of blood lends itself to telling a tale. Much of the story is interchangeable, allowing you your chance to be creative in the assembly of a poem.

Even novels are good sources for a found poem.

Example Using *The Great Gatsby*

Find phrases from within the novel to create a poem on one of the following aspects of *The Great Gatsby:*

Nick's character

Gatsby's character

Tom's character

Daisy's character

Jordan's character

Affluenza or illness resulting from materialism

The poem should be typed, double-spaced with twelve-point font, a title, and twenty to thirty lines. I usually give a 10% grade reduction for any format deviation. A sample rubric can be found on page 140.

The Found Story

Technically, this is far more challenging than the Found Poem assignment because of the depth of imagination required to create a story from a longer work. Before engaging in this assignment, you need to have a strong familiarity with the piece.

The Found Story assignment is ideal for longer works. As with the found poem, the found story can be an abridged reflection of the target text. The found story can work with plays as seen in Chapter Eleven: Cutting Drama and Humor. You can create a one-act play from a three- or five-act play.

The possibilities with the Found Story are numerous. What I have experienced success with is *The Grapes of Wrath* as a novel and Brian Friel's *Molly Sweeney* as a play. The reason why *The Grapes of Wrath* lends itself so well to the Found Story is because it's a story of a family in dire circumstances moving from Oklahoma to California. There are a variety of subplots that can be fused together to create a short story.

Molly Sweeney lends itself so well because it's about a young woman, having been born blind, through the marvel of modern medicine gains some sight — only to go blind again. This three-act play can be easily converted to a one-act play.

One strategy to start the Found Story assignment would be to copy several pages out of the targeted text. The way to select the page might be to look for the most dramatic elements and speeches. For example, in *The Grapes of Wrath* a dramatic scene would be when Ma Joad reflects on the burial of her mother and the disappearance of Noah. That could be the scene you build around to create the story, but you would still use the entire book.

There is an Example Assignment Sheet for *The Grapes of Wrath* on page 141, and for *Molly Sweeney* on page 141.

Chapter Twenty-Five:
The Vocabulary Skit

I believe the importance of vocabulary frees the mind. For years I taught vocabulary in the traditional manner where I would give tests, students would answer questions, and rarely would they retain the "learned" vocabulary. Once during a class evaluation, a student replied that he knew the importance of vocabulary, but the words went in one ear and out the other and there had to be a better way. On the value of this suggestion, I created the following section. This section demonstrates how to use vocabulary throughout an academic year.

Here you work in teams throughout a semester to complete a skit that you practice during the school week. The words selected are grouped from Latin prefixes and suffixes and Greek word elements. The reasoning behind this selection is that if you learn the Latin and Greek cognates, then you may be better equipped to speculate as to the meaning of words that have that cognate in them.

The small group presents a simple skit or sketch that contains ten vocabulary words in it. The first week is especially challenging because you only choose from the first ten words and therefore do not have much leeway to experiment with other words.

The quiz becomes cumulative weeks two through twelve as the small "vocabulary group" presents at least six words from the current week and as many as four words from the previous week. In other words, if your group presents weeks two through twelve, you need to use at least six words from the current list, but you could use seven or eight or even ten if you wanted. Whatever number you choose from in the current week, the balance must be from previous weeks and the total number of vocabulary words used must be ten.

The grading for your vocabulary skit is based on fifty points for those creating the skit and ten points for those taking the quiz. Students taking the quiz earn one half point for spelling and one half point for providing a proper definition. The students giving the quiz are graded on a fifty-point scale. If they spell and use the words correctly, each presenter receives all fifty points. If you miss one spelling or usage, you would lose two and a half points per error, be it spelling or usage. I do not take off for the creativity or lack thereof. But if you read the instructions carefully, you do have opportunities to earn extra credit if your group uses and identifies a literary term within your skit.

Throughout the week, the presenting group develops and types up the skit and highlights the vocabulary words. During the performance of the skit, presenting students should pause after stating a sentence with a vocabulary word in it. After the key vocabulary word is uttered, the rest of the class writes down the word they hear. I have the presenters go over their skit twice so that those who may have missed a word in the skit can have another opportunity to listen for it. That is the reason why I do not require the students to have all the words in the same order they were presented.

After the players have done the skit twice, you sit down, and the rest of the class has a few minutes to write down definitions. Another extra credit bonus is that if you are taking the test and correctly identify a literary term being used, you will receive an extra credit point.

You are encouraged to use the vocabulary words in your compositions and other investigations throughout the year. I offer up to five points per essay of extra credit, one point for each vocabulary word used. I limit the number of words you can use for extra credit because you need to develop your own style and voice without being too encumbered with the possibility of limitless extra credit.

A sample assignment handout can be found on page 142.

Chapter Twenty-Six:
The Storyboard – Make the Drama

A storyboard is a great way for you to work on translating what you read into another medium. Ask yourself, "How do books and stories transform into plays? What visuals could be useful to produce a movie from a book?" The answers formerly locked from you will be magically opened in this chapter on storyboards. If you have the opportunity to create a script or a movie from a novel or short story, this section will show you two different ways to make that happen: in a group and individually.

Group Storyboard

With the group storyboard you will create a visual and scripted version of a book within a group. The teacher will divide the book into sections, assigning each group a section. Follow the steps in the group and you will see how to manage a project where everyone within the group has different tasks. Each group has a couple of different responsibilities. Half the group can work on the art of the board, while the other half works on the dialogue.

In the next part of this version, members from the groups need to work with members assigned the same task from other groups in order for the project to work. The end result should be a seamless presentation of a story by the entire class. So those who work on the artistic representation need to get with other groups' members assigned to the art task. You need to make sure that you don't needlessly repeat what the other group is doing. The same is true of the scriptwriters. If you are in the script group, meet with the scriptwriters from the other groups in order to have smooth, seamless transitions from segment to segment. A sample assignment handout and rubric can be found on page 144.

Individual Storyboard

The following is from Joey DeStefano, another great colleague in the English Department at Heritage High School.

This individual storyboard is an assignment where you work with only a few paragraphs of a selected work and dive into the interpretations of a selection. Here you uncover cinematography and choreograph photos and/or pictures to capture a scene.

110

Before you begin and get introduced to the story in a picture format, it is important to draw a scene as you see it. To do that, you will need to know these terms:

1. *scene*: a selected series of pictures and/or dialogue from a part of a screenplay
2. *shot*: a selected series of frames from within a scene
   a. *pan:* how the angle of a camera moves from one side to another
   b. *zoom:* how the camera moves in to get a closer look at something within the shot
   c. *tilt:* vertical pivot
   d. *dolly:* camera on a track to follow action; in other words, the camera moves — not pan.
3. *frame:* any pause or still from within a shot

Your task is to watch a scene from a favorite show, identify it, and note how the above terms relate to it. Then fill out the Show Analysis Worksheet on page 145.

On your own piece of paper, identify another scene using the model from above. This time *draw* the frame exactly as you see it.

More movie jargon:

angle: the degree at which the action is shot

depth: the focus of the action up front (foreground) versus background

color manipulation: the sharpness of color, black and white

shot selection and literary connection: is there a symbol in the background?

In order to write a storyboard, take the scene you have selected or the class has viewed, and do the following on your own sheet of paper:

1. First frame of each shot is drawn separately
2. Dialogue is written underneath the frame in which it occurs
3. When the camera moves, the first and last frame of the shot are drawn separately and the movement of the camera is explained between the boxes on the margin.

Now, take this exercise one step further and increase the number of shots from three to six. You can minimize the shots and arrange one or two extra camera movements. Consider how the increase of shots and camera movements alter the scene.

Once you understand a little bit about how a scene works, it is time to work from within a written piece. Select what you consider to be an important section of a book or short story. The selection should be short — a few paragraphs. The next section is to convert the text to image via the storyboard. Try to include a symbol that is an object that has more meaning than its physical value.

After you have completed your storyboard, reflect upon how you created it. In your reflection write the following:

1. Rational: Explain what you intended to show through your storyboard. Answer the questions, "What have I achieved? How have I achieved it?"

2. Response: What was difficult about transferring text to image? What was impossible? Did you like the assignment? Was it effective? Why or why not?

3. Analysis: Write down what you actually think is meant by the expressions, "I like movies better than books," and "I like books better than movies."

4. Discussion: Consider with your mates as to whether or not a movie should aim at accuracy or creativity in interpretation when representing a novel, play, short story, or historical event.

5. Film: If possible, create a movie with your storyboard and present it to the class. Write a reflection about the challenges and limitations.

Chapter Twenty-Seven:
The Group Story

Another example from the excellent teaching practices of Joseph DeStefano comes in the form of the Group Story. In this activity you will create all kinds of stories based on your knowledge of specific plot structure. Ideally, you will all get into groups of five.

To begin, review the most common five elements of a typical story. The first element is the *setting*. It is in the setting where the basic geographic and physical locations are situated and the main characters are introduced. It is in the setting when the author can use the literary term of *foreshadow* to hint to something upcoming within the story. The second part of the story is the *rising action*. It is during the rising action that tensions become more apparent. The conflict of the story becomes evident here. Any influences from the setting become further developed in the rising action as well. The third part of the story is the *climax*. It is in the climax where all the energy is focused. All the building tension comes out front and center. Maybe this is where a cleverly inserted foreshadow becomes apparent. The fourth segment of a story is called the *falling action,* a fancier word for it is *denouement,* the French word for "unraveling" or "untying." It is here where the reader realizes the results of the climax. The fifth and final segment of the story is the *resolution*. This part prepares the reader for the end of the story. In terms of the climax and falling action, it is here where all mysteries are resolved.

Your role is to write on each segment of a story given five minutes for each section. The desks should be arranged as illustrated. When you begin, everyone writes on the setting and begins a story. After you write for five minutes, you stop and pass your paper up. The first person passes his or her paper back to the last person in the row. Then the class writes on the rising action for five minutes, and then everyone passes his or her paper up. The process is repeated until we end with the completed story. Each row should have five completed stories. All group members should review each completed story. Then each group decides a favorite of the five to share with the class.

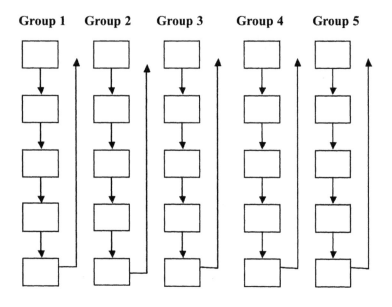

Chapter Twenty-Eight:
Class Discussion

Class discussions are an important part of learning the value of others' thoughts concerning a common issue. What makes a class discussion so special? It is unique and absolutely flexible. You can cover practically any topic through carefully orchestrated classroom discussions.

There are four types of class discussions included in this chapter. The first is the basic class discussion where you discuss a class topic based on who has the answer. The next is the circle-in-a-circle discussion. The third is bringing a friend into the discussion. The last type of discussion is the focus group prepared discussion.

Who Has the Answer?

The first and simplest type of discussion is the basic *who has the answer?* Here you respond to prompts. These can be in the form of questions asked directly to the class or statements concerning a subject or issue the class has covered. Often, this type of dialogue can be used not only to review a chapter or topic, but also to preview the next chapter or section of the class. For example, if you think that a certain passage is a potential foreshadow, you can infer, or read between the lines, and guess what might happen next. You can liven up a class discussion by bringing your own prompts and questions coming from your notes.

Circle-in-a-Circle

The next type of discussion is a *circle-in-a-circle* discussion. This type of discussion can be lively. First, there are five or six students selected to sit in a circle. The other students encircle the chosen five or six. Only the six may speak. They can speak to one of the prepared prompts or another idea or question they have about the material.

The other students enter by tapping a student in the discussion group. The tapped students leave and are replaced by the incoming participant. The student new to the group has the floor and begins a discussion. You can continue to participate, even if you are tapped out by tapping in and reentering the discussion group. The goal is for the whole class to contribute.

Bring a Friend

The next form of class discussion is the *bring a friend* discussion. First, on a piece of paper you will write a question or come up with a discussion topic. Your teacher may give you a specific topic to write on. Then you are to write your name on a separate piece of paper. Keep your prompt, but place your piece of paper with your name in a pile with the other names. Your teacher may choose to use a hat to collect all the names. Then you randomly select names, making sure you do not get your own, and the discussion begins. A student starts by asking their prompt to the named student on the card they pulled. The student asking the question to his or her mate gets credit and the student answering receives credit. If the named student cannot answer, another student can interject and earn participation points. Even if you can't answer the question destined for you, you might be able to recapture that missing credit by participation in the ensuing discussion. The targeted student, whether they could answer the question or not, then asks a question to the student whose card he or she has received.

You continue in this fashion until the entire class has asked their questions. You are not restricted to the prompts your mates come up with; you can react to another's answer and continue with a free flow of ideas.

Focus Group

The *focus group* class discussion is another way for you to celebrate what you have recently learned. Here, you form groups of five or six. In these groups, you have one question. It may be a question pertaining to a cited quotation. You each relate the answer to another quotation that you individually find. Each student finds a quotation different from others in the group. This is where you must communicate with each other and select different quotations. It takes about fifteen minutes for you to come up with answers and then you each will present your findings. Here you learn to thematically connect your ideas.

Chapter Twenty-Nine:
Protest Poetry

This chapter is where you learn that the spark of artistic genius is often a result of external pressure. You look at various aspects of rebellion in society. What institutions are in need of change? Ask yourself what isn't working correctly and — more importantly — how do you know this aspect of society is not working?

You will get into groups and discuss what isn't working in society. Sometimes, you may have difficulties with your parents. Some may have problems with the structure of school or curfew laws or any one of a number of problems in society. In this section you will have the chance to identify with artists whose protests against societal institutions emerge in their work. Ultimately, you will then analyze the literature, poem, song, or painting and explain how you know that it is a protest.

The following is a step-by-step guide to protest poetry.

Activity One

Name a piece of literature that you identify with the protest. Think of song lyrics, books, news articles, etc. What does it protest? What is the overall message? Do you agree with the protest? Also, name an institution that you feel is being challenged by some aspect of society. Why do you feel that this institution faces criticism? What do you think will result from the pressure?

Activity Two

Share your literature, thoughts, and feelings with members of the class. Answer the question, "What mood does this piece of work convey?" Ask classmates if they agree.

Presentations

Here you will choose between three categories for your presentation, each one with increasing difficulty and point value.

Category One – 50 Points

Category One Option One: Students present poetry or other medium such as music and write a 500-word description as to how the piece reveals protest.

Category One Option Two: Students organize a presentation on three significant occurrences during the year of their birth. Explain how you know these events are significant. What are the impacts of these incidences? At least 500 words analyze the three events.

Category One Option Three: Students compile a current American event as described by three articles in the newspaper or magazines. The review of the event needs to include a summary of the event and a prognosis of what will happen in the future. How might the event inspire future artists?

Category One Option Four: Other presentations include analyzing a work of art that demonstrates protest of an issue or situation with a 500-word written analysis.

Category Two – 75 Points

Category Two Option One: Students vary a presentation with either a musical instrument or some other creative medium that is delivered in class. For example, the student could identify an area of protest through the performance. A 500-word analysis follows or previews the performance.

Category Two Option Two: The students could act a scene, either created or reenacted, that illustrates the concept of protest. The students then need to deliver an analysis illustrating how they know that the scene exhibits some form of protest. The scene is two and a half minutes for a solo performance and five minutes for a duet. The analysis must be typed and presented in at least 500 words.

Category Three – 100 Points

Category Three Option: The student presents a PowerPoint or electronic presentation detailing an era of protest. The student includes music, poetry, history, and any other important aspects of the protest he or she desires. A one-thousand-word analysis accompanies the performance.

Other options include an original poem or performance with analysis for fifty, seventy-five, or 100 points. Value is based on your effort.

Students can mix and match poems, songs, and current articles with a PowerPoint presentation for seventy-five to 100 points depending on effort put forth. Students select the value.

Chapter Thirty:
Essay Workshop and Gallery

This activity is great for comparing two works. The class is divided into groups based on essay topic interest. First, you need to have a long piece of butcher paper and at least two different colored markers. Put the topic across the top, and then underneath the topic draw a line down the center. On each side of the line, write the titles of the books you are comparing.

Once you have your topic written on top and titles on either side of the line, start researching quotations from the text that are relevant to your topic. Write down the quotations in one color and your analysis in another color. Make sure the analysis has something to do with both the topic and the other selection. Do this for both sides of the paper. Draw lines where quotations can directly compare. When you have exhausted your resources from the target texts, put up your paper in the classroom. Now, you are ready for the Essay Gallery.

Once all groups have hung their papers, you can then look at each other's work. Take a notebook and write down the quotations and analysis that might help you write your essay.

The following steps may help you get started:

1. Students get into groups based on essay interest.
2. Students work with magic markers to include quotations, lead-ins, and analysis.
3. Work is created on the large construction paper.
4. If you are doing a pro/con, or comparison essay format, write a line in the middle of the page to show that there are two distinct sides.
5. Use quotations in full.
6. Analyze the quotation. Explain how it matches the ideas presented.

Forms, Worksheets, and Handouts

Class Expectations and Guidelines
Fundamentals of Speech

School Materials
Pencil or pen – 50 cents; spiral notebook – $2; learning to speak in front of others without losing your nerve – priceless!

Welcome to the Heritage High School Speech program! Your choice to enter into the world of public and interpretive speaking is an excellent one. This class introduces you to the world of public speaking.

As we meet Tuesdays and Thursdays, you will find that this course moves along very quickly. Get with your mates if you miss class! Assignments are geared toward the next class session.

Attendance/Makeup Policy
Students who have an excused absence will be given two working days to make up missing work. Students who have an unexcused absence will not be able to recapture missing credit. Students can submit work in the make up basket designated "Speech" on the filing cabinet next to my desk in the Language Arts office. Occasionally, tardies happen to the best of us. Excessive tardiness will draw the customary detention/school cleanup. Try to get here on time.

General Information
This course is designed to be a fun learning experience. Homework sets the tempo for the next class. A conscientious job guarantees success.

Goals
You will have experience with the following concepts in speech:
• Develop fluency in speaking style
• Understanding a strategy for verbally supporting your ideas
• A knowledge of the organization and workings of a group
• Understanding how to carry yourself when delivering a speech
• Develop confidence with a practiced speaking tone

Behavior Expectations
The class follows the rules and guidelines listed in your student handbook. If general courtesy and common sense are not obvious to you, I will make the necessary adjustments. My office hours are: 2nd and 5th every day; 2nd, 5th, 6th, and 7th MWF as of this writing. Feel free to drop by or use the sign-up sheet on the filing cabinet in front of my desk. Finally, speaking in front of a large group frightens some, there are others who have no problem speaking in public, and others who may speak too much! This course seeks to extend the confidence to those who are quiet, reinforce the skills of those who are comfortable, and help to control those who speak a little too much.

3-D Collage Rubric

Introduction – 10 points possible
9 – 10 points: Introduction is creative and sets the mood for the whole of the piece.
8 points: Introduction misses part of the above criteria.
7 or less: Introduction misses much of the criteria listed above.

Visual Aid – 20 points possible
18 – 20: Visual is original and covered in detail for the whole presentation.
16 – 17: Visual lacks an important component for the presentation.
15 or less: Visual does not reflect the preparation needed for this part of the assignment.

Overall Presentation – 20 points possible
18 – 20: The presentation provides the audience with an understanding into the speaker. The presentation is rehearsed and competently delivered to the class. The student meets the time requirements.
16 – 17: The presentation provides the audience with a sense of who the speaker is. The presentation is not polished, yet preparation is evident. The student meets the time requirements.
14 – 15: The speaker has minimal preparation. The speaker is unclear with some of the information presented. The presentation follows basic instruction. The student does not meet the time requirements.
13 or less: Not much preparation is evident. The speaker does not follow instructions. The student does not meet the time requirements.

Interview Activity Rubric

The time requirement for the interview is from three to five minutes. Therefore, we will spend time in class developing your interviews.

Interviewer Rubric
18 – 20: The interviewer clearly asks questions and includes follow-up questions when needed for clarification. Time requirements are met.
16 – 17: The interviewer misses an obvious follow-up question. The time requirements may be short.
15 or less: The interviewer lacks several of the above criteria.

Subject Response Rubric
18 – 20: The subject responds to all questions clearly. The interaction makes it clear that the pair has practiced the interview. The time requirements are met.
16 – 17: The subject is not clear or practiced with all responses. Time requirements are not met.
15 or less: The subject lacks several of the above criteria.

Student Comment Sheet

Name _____

Remember to keep all comments constructive!

Introduction
There is a clear attention-getting device. There is a preview of points.

Comments: _____
_____
_____
_____

Content
The speaker elaborates on each previewed point. The visual works well to develop the speech. Research is evident on all the points. The speaker uses transitions to help the speech flow.

Comments: _____
_____
_____
_____

Delivery
The speaker uses hand gestures effectively. When not gesturing, the hands remain at the sides, relaxed with the elbows slightly bent. The speaker has few if any verbal pauses. The speaker varies voice tone and pacing. The speaker maintains eye contact with the audience at all times. The speaker moves to include the entire class in the speech.

Comments: _____
_____
_____
_____

Conclusion
The speaker reviews the main points covered.

Comments: _____
_____
_____
_____

Demonstration Speech Scoring Guide

Name_____

Please present this guide to the instructor before giving your speech.

Introduction
18 – 20: The speaker introduces the speech effectively. The speaker uses a concise preview of points that flows directly into the body of the speech.
16 – 17: The speaker misses one of the above criteria in the speech. The opening of the speech leads into the main points.
Under 16: The information presented in the introduction lacks significant portions of the introductory criteria.

Content
36 – 40: The speaker elaborates on each point. Research is evident on each point. The speech flows evenly with transitions.
32 – 35: The speaker elaborates on each point. Research is not evident on each point.
31 or less: The speaker may not elaborate on each point. The research is shoddy.

Delivery
18 – 20: The speaker uses hand gestures effectively. When not gesturing, the hands remain at the sides, relaxed with the elbows slightly bent. The speaker has few if any verbal pauses. The speaker varies voice tone and pacing. The speaker maintains eye contact with the audience at all times. The speaker moves to include the entire class in the speech.
16 – 17: The speaker misses one of the criteria mentioned above.
15 or less: The speaker misses more than one of the criteria stated above.

Conclusion
9 – 10: The speaker reviews all stated points.
Under 9: The speaker does not review the stated points.

Presence
10: The speaker dresses for the part. Men wear a jacket and tie. Women wear a long dress, skirt, or dress pants with a blouse. *If you do not have these garments, see me in advance and arrangements will be made.

Demonstration Speech Worksheet

Attention-Getting Device: _____

_____

_____

_____

Preview of Points: _____

_____

_____

_____

Use of Visual/Elaboration of Points: _____

_____

_____

_____

_____

_____

Conclusion/Review of Points: _____

_____

_____

_____

Broadcast News Worksheet

1. Briefly explain the format of your news program.

_____

_____

_____

_____

_____

2. What are all your group members planning to do? Write a brief summary of their parts in the space below.

_____

_____

_____

_____

_____

3. How are you planning to organize the broadcast? Provide a brief narrative as to what will happen during the show.

_____

_____

_____

_____

_____

_____

Evening News Rubric

45 – 50: All members contribute equally. Everyone participates and takes their time
responsibility. There is an anchor who facilitates between various reports and
reporters along with speaking on the top stories. Each member is prepared and
reports on an issue or issues within their subject.
40 – 44: A key component is missing or the group does not make the time requirement.
39 or less: More than one key component is missing.

Sports Broadcast Worksheet

Describe the situation: _____

_____

_____

_____

_____

Play-by-play synopsis: _____

_____

_____

_____

_____

_____

_____

Color synopsis: _____

_____

_____

_____

_____

_____

_____

Sports Broadcast Rubric

45 – 50: The team meets the time requirement. The performance is balanced. The team
presents the situation in a realistic format. Rehearsal is evident.
40 – 44: The team misses one of the above criteria.
39 or less: The team misses more than one of the above criteria.

Speech Commercial Worksheet

1. Briefly explain the product you intend to promote.

_____

_____

_____

_____

2. What are your group members planning to do? Write a brief summary of their parts in the
space below.

_____

_____

_____

_____

3. How are you planning to organize the commercial? Provide a brief narrative as to what
will happen during the commercial.

_____

_____

_____

_____

Commercial Rubric

18 – 20: The students had a catchy phrase, jingle, or clever dialogue to show the need or effect of the product. All students brought a prop. It was clear to the audience what was being marketed and the purpose of the product.

16 – 17: The group misses one of the above criteria

15 or less: The group misses more than one of the above criteria.

Grading Criteria for Debate over the Issues

45 – 50:

1. Students present and refute case using signpost language. For example, point/subpoint language is used and clearly indicates the flow of the debate.

2. The students each speak for at least one minute. The rebuttal explains how the points work in the debate.

3. Each side brings up the points from the other side. Each side explains why they win the debate.

4. Use of evidence is effective.

23 – 26: One of the criteria is missing.

22 or less: More than one of the criteria is missing.

Public Forum Worksheet

The (affirmative/negative) teams stand firmly against/for the resolution _____

_____

_____

_____

The following (use about three or four main points) reasons bolster our position. (State a preview of points and remember to signpost your language.)

_____

_____

_____

_____

The first reason why the resolution should be (affirmed/refuted) is: (The following represents the research and logical reasoning behind the first previewed point. After the logical analysis, be sure to reiterate the resolution and why this analysis supports your view.)

_____

_____

_____

_____

The second reason why the resolution should be (affirmed/refuted) is: (The following represents the research and logical reasoning behind the first previewed point. After the logical analysis, be sure to reiterate the resolution and why this analysis supports your view).

_____

_____

_____

_____

Team A	Team B
Notes on opening remarks:	Notes on opening remarks:
Notes on crossfire:	Notes on crossfire:
Notes on Speaker 2:	Notes on Speaker 2:
Notes on crossfire:	
Notes on summary Speaker 1:	Notes on summary Speaker 2:
Notes on grand crossfire:	
Notes on last shot Speaker 2:	Notes on last shot Speaker 2:

Reason for decision: _____

_____

_____

Congress Speech Rubric and Scoring Guide

Introduction

18 – 20: The speaker uses an attention-getting device to open the speech. The preview of points follows the AGD. The speaker clearly states his or her opinion on the topic. The speaker illustrates the reasons, or a preview of points, why that side of the issue should be maintained. The speaker sells his or her side of the resolution to the congress.

17 or less: The speaker misses one or more of the above criteria.

Body

14 – 15: The speaker elaborates on the previewed points. Research is cited for each of the points. Transitions help to segue between points. Each point connects directly to the issue at hand.

13 or less: The speaker misses at least one of the criteria.

Conclusion

14 – 15: The speaker reviews the points. The speaker ends by selling his or her side of the resolution. The speaker meets the minimum time requirement.

13 or less: The speaker misses at least one of the criteria.

Congress Speech Worksheet

Attention-Getting Device _____

_____

_____

Stance on Resolution _____

_____

_____

Preview of Points _____

_____

_____

_____

_____

Body of Speech_____

_____

_____

_____

_____

_____

_____

_____

Conclusion _____

_____

_____

_____

Oratory Prep Sheet

Attention-getter (Interesting quotation, anecdote, scenario, or daunting statistic).

_____

_____

_____

Lead-in to thesis or main point.

_____

_____

_____

Preview of points. Explain some universal appeal here in a few areas of analysis.

_____

_____

_____

Elaboration of points, in order of preview. Facts as presented by research go here.

_____

_____

_____

Conclusion leading back to the original attention-getter and repeating the main point.

_____

_____

_____

Extemporaneous Prep Sheet

Attention-getter (Interesting quotation, anecdote, scenario, or daunting statistic).

_____

_____

_____

Lead-in to question repeated verbatim.

_____

_____

_____

Preview of points.

_____

_____

_____

Elaboration of points, in order of preview.

_____

_____

_____

Conclusion leading back to the original attention-getter and answering the question.

_____

_____

_____

Extemporaneous Prep Sheet Pro/Con Format

Attention-getter (Interesting quotation, anecdote, scenario, or daunting statistic).

_____

_____

_____

Lead-in to question repeated verbatim.

_____

_____

_____

Preview of points.

For Side A

_____

_____

_____

For Side B

_____

_____

_____

Elaboration of points (in order of preview).
Side A   Side B

_____   _____

_____   _____

_____   _____

_____   _____

Conclusion leading back to the original attention-getter and answering the question.

_____

_____

_____

Extemporaneous Prep Sheet Problem/Solution

Attention-getter (Interesting quotation, anecdote, scenario, or daunting statistic).

_____

_____

_____

Lead-in to question repeated verbatim.

_____

_____

_____

Preview of points: Factors creating the problem/solution solving the problem.

_____

_____

_____

Elaboration of points (in order of preview).

Factors Creating Problem   Solution Alleviating Problem

_____   _____

_____   _____

_____   _____

_____   _____

Conclusion leading back to the original attention-getter and answering the question.

_____

_____

_____

Lincoln-Douglas Debate Worksheet

Attention-Getting Device (use either a daunting statistic, an interesting scenario, or a pertinent quotation) Because I believe these words by _____, I stand firmly resolved _____(for/against) the resolution (stated verbatim) _____

To clarify today's debate, I offer the following definitions. (Key terms in the resolution are defined here.)

My value in today's debate will be _____, supported by the criterion of _____

My first contention is _____

Subpoint A is (This demonstrates a practical example of how the contention works in real world situations.)

My second contention is _____

Subpoint A is (This demonstrates a practical example of how the contention works in real world situations.)

Rubric and Scoring Guide for Readers Theatre

Performance

18 – 20: Roles were evenly dispersed. Students were well rehearsed. Students met the time
criterion. There was an informative introduction.

16 – 17: One of the above criteria was missing.

15 or less: More than one of the above criteria was missing.

Analysis

9 – 10: The group shows the author's intent, relates their scene to the piece, and describes
the importance of the scene to today's world.

7 – 8: The group misses one of the above criteria.

6 or less: More than one of the above criteria was missing.

Props

9 – 10: All group members bring a recognizable prop.

7 – 8: One member forgets his or her prop.

Readers Theatre Worksheet

Briefly describe the scene you are preparing:

_____

_____

Explain who is doing what in this scene and analysis.

_____

_____

_____

_____

Write out the text of what you are going to say in the presentation.

_____

_____

_____

_____

_____

_____

_____

_____

_____

Choral Reading Rubric

45 – 50: All players know their roles and contribute to the success of the performance. Each
      player brings a prop or costume that enhances the project. Interpretation is
      evident. Rehearsal practice and coordination perfect in this performance.

40 – 44: Players understand their roles, but miss at least one criteria of the performance.

39 or less: Players lack a considerable portion of the interpretation.

Scoring Guide for the Salem Witch Trial

27 – 30: Each side supports its case using quotations from the play. Each student in the
      defense or prosecution side leaves a written summary of their facts. The judges
      explain the reasons for their decision in a half-page paragraph. Time requirements
      are used.

23 – 26: One of the above criteria is missing.

22 and less: More than one of the above criteria are missing.

Rubric for the Trial of Henry Fleming for Desertion

36 – 40: The paper and presentation clearly state the student's position. The author uses at
      least one quotation from the text to illustrate the point. Handwriting is clear and
      easy to read. There is a minimum of two spelling or punctuation errors.

32 – 35: The paper and presentation state the writer's position. The author uses at least
      one quotation from the text to illustrate the point. Handwriting is clear and easy to
      read. There may be more than two spelling errors, or the paper lacks other criteria.

31 and less: The paper misses several of the above criteria.

Rubric for the Body Sculpture Activity

The passage was identified and was typed: 10 points
The theme identified and supported in at least 500 words: 20 points
The format is twelve-point font and double-spaced: 5
There is a works cited section: 5

Rubric for the Found Poem

27 – 30: Poem meets the requirements of being typed, double-spaced with twelve-point
      font, a title, and twenty to thirty lines. Phrases are well considered and flow well.

23 – 26: Poem misses one requirement. The poem is conscientiously put together.

22 or less: The poem misses more than one requirement.

Example Assignment Sheet for *The Grapes of Wrath*

In this assignment, the student creates a short story from the novel. The purpose is for the student to experience how to create a story by arranging sentences into paragraphs, thus creating a short story out of the sentences that Steinbeck uses in his novel. Students should use the entirety of the novel to complete the story. The purpose is to create something while having fun with the story being studied.

Feel free to use whole paragraphs as long as they move along the story you intend to tell. Some story ideas include:

• The fall of an American family

• The conquest of evil

• The indomitable American spirit

• The plight of women

• The Great Depression

• Hope

Choose one of these ideas or a pre-approved idea of your own, and photocopy no less than seven pages from the text to serve as the foundation for your piece. Highlight where you used the specific lines for your story and have that photocopied page attached to your story. Attach the pages in the order of the story. In other words, the pages do not have to be written in the chronology of the text, just the order in which your story is set. Make sure that it is typed, 12-point font, and a minimum of 2 to 3 pages in length.

Scoring Guide:
45 – 50: The writer meets all of the above criteria and the chronology coheres logically.
40 – 44: The writer misses one of the above criteria and/or has mistyped a line and the
        piece is not the required length.
39 or less: The writer misses more than one of the criteria.

Example Assignment Sheet for *Molly Sweeney*

In this assignment, the students find a short story within the play *Molly Sweeney*. The play follows the "Flowers for Algernon" theme where young Molly gains sight for the first time only to lose it. Here you can create a smaller story within the play. You can create scenes that may have the story follow along as a story-within-the-story type of setting. Here you can be creative and reverse the fortunes of Molly by having her gain her sight and finish your dialogue there. As the writer of a play, be sure to include stage directions that reflect the story you are telling. Make sure you keep the dialogue consistent with the situation.

The criteria are as follows:
45 – 50: The writer creates one scene with stage direction and coherent text placement that
        is at least two pages in length. There is a story told and the audience understands
        that the story comes to a logical conclusion.
40 – 44: The writer misses one of the above criteria.
39 or less: The writer misses more than one of the above criteria.

141

Vocabulary Skit Explanation Handout

Each week one group will either volunteer or be selected to present the vocabulary quiz. This group will use ten vocabulary words in a situation. Situations can vary. Test days are usually Thursdays. Instead of participating in the silent sustained reading period that week, those students will work on creating their skit to be performed the following Thursday.

Students get to perform these skits at least two times per semester. In the first quiz, students use all ten vocabulary words. In the following tests, students use at least six words from that week's list and as many as four words from previous lists. The hardest part about making a skit is to create a situation where all the words will work. Students who participate in the actual skit receive a grade based on a 50-point scale. They receive no grade on the quiz. Students taking the quizzes are graded on a 10-point scale. The group grades are added in at the end of the semester. The class taking the test will be graded on spelling and understanding. The group presenting the skit will be graded on proper usage and spelling.

The vocabulary group presents the skit and gives the instructor a typed copy of the script before the presentation. All of the vocabulary words are underlined or otherwise highlighted. While presenting, students act out the scene. The rest of the class writes down the vocabulary words as they hear them. The words do not have to be in the order of the presentation. After someone finishes a sentence with a vocabulary word in it, the players pause for a silent count of three. That gives the class time to write down the word. Usually, the group will perform the skit two times in a semester. Some successful skit examples: Scooby-Doo, Survivor, Elimidate, Nightly News, Courtroom Scene, American Idol, Fear Factor, Cops and Robbers, What's My Line, Cafeteria Gossip, The Abercrombie Girl, Play-by-Play Sports Event, Aliens Attack, etc. Have fun in coming up with a creative idea for this skit. Students get four reading periods to develop the skit. The first day the students should come up with an idea. If the group has any questions concerning usage, please ask.

*Extra credit bonus: Five extra credit points will be awarded to the group that uses a literary term in their skit. The group needs to identify the literary term used. And one extra credit point is awarded to any class member who identifies a literary term being used during the presentation.

If it appears that, for whatever reason, we cannot perform a skit, no worries, I have many traditional tests available for use.

Latin Prefixes

Week 1	Week 2	Week 3	Week 4	Week 5
ab, a , abs – from	ante- before	semi – half	extra – outside	interlude
abdicate	antecedents	semimonthly	extracurricular	il, im, ir - not
abduct	ante meridiem	semiannual	extraneous	illegible
abhor	post – after	e, ex – out	intra – within	illiterate
abscond	postdate	enervate	intramural	impunity
avert	postgraduate	emigrate	intrastate	incessant
ad – toward	post meridiem	evoke	contro, counter-	irrelevant
advent	postscript	expel	against	bene - good
adapt	bi – two	in,	controversy	benediction
adherent	bimonthly	imminent	contraband	benefactor
adverse	bilateral	implicate	contravene	mal - bad
addicted	bisect	impugn	countermand	malediction
		insurgent	inter – between	malevolent
			intercede	

Week 6	Week 7	Week 8	Week 9	Week 10
se – apart	concord	per - through	am, amor – love	flu, fluc, flux – flow
secede	convene	perennial	amorous	fluctuate
sedition	coherent	perplex	amiable	fluid
seclude	ob – against	permeate	amity	influx
segregate	obliterate	persist	enamored	gen, gener – birth, class
circum – around	obviate	pertinent	anim – mind, will	
circumlocution	obsess	perturb	animosity	degenerate
circumnavigate	pre – before	pro – forward	equanimity	engender
circumspect	precede	prominent	magnanimous	genre

Week 6	Week 7	Week 8	Week 9	Week 10
circumvent	preclude	profuse	fin – end, limit	regenerate
co, col – together with	procrastinate	affinity		greg – gather, flock
coalesce	precocious	propel	definitive	aggregate
collusion	preface		finale	congregation
				gregarious

Week 11	Week 12
here, – stick	manu – hand
adhere	emancipate
cohere	mandate
inherent	pend, pens - hang
lateral – side	append
collateral	impending
unilateral	pending
multilateral	suspend
luc, lum – light	suspense
elucidate	pon, pos - put
lucid	depose
luminary	impose
illuminate	transpose

Latin Roots

Week 13	Week 14	Week 15	Week 16	Week 17	Week 18
superfluous	annihilation	comely	cumbersome	scrib, write	sol, lonely
imperfection	Short-sighted	unscrupulous	barrage	conscript	desolate
wagers	severity	hesitation	oblivious	inscription	sole
beneficial	development	meticulous	unscrupulous	prescribe	soliloquy
outmoded	deterioration	spasmodic	Impending	scribe	solitude
abnormalities	responsive	controversy	endeavors	subscribe	solo
delusions	ambitious	dispute	illumined	simil, like	solv, loosen
milestones	unrivaled	contraction	ascend	assimilate	solvent
reductions	impenetrable	modification	retrieve	dissimilar	dissolution
long-term	arrogant	rejection	deluded	simile	resolution
dejected	strenuous	hindrance	dispense	simultaneous	soluble
verisimilitude	absolute				

Week 19	Week 20	Week 21	Week 22	Week 23
Unda, wave	vid, vis, see	cracy, belief	perpetual	integrity
Abound	envision	autocracy	sublime	manifest
Abundant	improvise	aristocracy	admonishing	proportionate
Inundate	revise	bureaucracy	manifold	pertinent
Redound				
Redundant				

Greek Word Elements

plutocracy	indubitably	encumbrance	auto, self	technocracy
integrate	impervious	Ver: true	authentic	dem, demo, people
blithe	temporal	Aver	autocrat	demagogue
occult	effete	Veracity	automaton	democracy
transcendent	incessantly	Verdict	autonomous	pan, panto, all
aversion	derision	Verify	automation	pantomime
veritable	autopsy	pandemic	Pandemonium	

Sample Assignment Handout for *The Sound of Waves* Storyboard Project

Art Part

Each group uses two 2' x 3' cardboard backed sections for the storyboard. Students may create symbols, scenery, or other visually pertinent depictions.

Thematic Part

Each group describes how the theme develops through the story. They can use ideas relative to the story. For example, the small-town mentality can be discussed. The idea of a preordained destiny or predetermined life can be discussed. Furthermore, the mores of a culture can be explored. The assignment follows a typical essay format where there is a three-paragraph requirement. The introductory paragraph is where the main ideas are presented. The second paragraph is where you write your evidence in the form of a quotation. Remember to give a lead-in to your evidence explaining where the quotation is coming from in the story. If someone is thinking or speaking, who is doing this and what is the situation? After the quotation, be sure to show how the quotation proves your point in an analysis following the evidence.

The Narrative Part

Here the students simply reduce the story to the necessary terms and create a small script that matches the storyboard. Dialogue and role play work to convey the meaning of Yukio Mishima's story.

The groups are divided chronologically: group 1 to page 32; group 2 to page 64; group 3 to page 95; group 4 to page 119; group 5 to page 146; group 6 to end.

How the Groups Work Together

Members from the groups who are doing the artistic part make sure that they have similar materials for each section of the storyboard. They know what the other groups are doing so as not to unnecessarily duplicate scenes. The analysis works with the scenes so that there is unity between the artwork and the thematic explanation. The script used in the narrative sequence follows both the artistic presentation and the analytic explanation. In other words, one can see through the script that the theme is illustrated and the art is followed.

The Sections of the Board are Consistent

The top part has the art, the middle has script, and the bottom has the analysis. The script and the analysis can be either written on the board itself in clear, legible writing, or cut and pasted on the boards.

Rubric

45 – 50: The student meets the above criteria. The contribution directly reflects the duties outlined above.

40 – 44: The student misses some part of the assignment, either in effort or another aspect.

39 or less: The student's effort misses more than one element of the assignment.

Show Analysis Worksheet

Scene: (describe the movie's or show's scene)

_____

_____

_____

Shot: (remember to include camera positions A through D as necessary to the shot)

_____

_____

_____

Frame:

_____

_____

_____

Appendix B:
Notes to the Teacher

Section One: Getting Started

Chapter One: The First Day and Breaking the Ice

A Positive First Day

Other good ideas to help set the mood for a positive first day experience:

- Welcome each student with a friendly handshake.
- Make sure to have students do something immediately upon entering the room.
- When they are seated, I pass around a blank seating chart and they fill it out. You may want to create a seating chart before the students get to class. In any case, a seating chart is valuable for classroom management, learning student names, and assisting substitutes.
- Present them with cards so they can start filling out their names once they are seated. I collect their cards and select students to read aloud segments of the course expectations and guidelines after mixing the cards. This activity has a couple of different purposes. On one hand, it gives the students a chance to ask questions about the specifics of the overall class expectations. Furthermore, you get a diagnostic as to how well students in the class can read and speak. It should take a class of twenty-five to thirty students ten to fifteen minutes to get seated and read the course guidelines and expectations.

After you go over the course expectations, the students need to have some sort of homework assignment designed to get each one in front of the class. After the homework assignment, my class usually plays a game. See Section One: Getting Started for ideas.

The Card Game

After collecting and remixing the cards, you can call on volunteers or simply randomly select students to name as many of their peers as possible. You could assign points based on how many facts the student gets right. You can extend the game to get a second-place winner, and so on. You could assign participation points if you use a participation scale. This game takes about twenty minutes.

Nonverbal Game of Human Communications

This game can be played at the beginning of the course or during the instruction on the importance of nonverbal communication. This takes about ten to fifteen minutes.

Liar

I don't attach a grade to this game, just a few extra credit points to the winners. This game could take thirty to forty-five minutes depending on class size.

Um

You time each student and award the longest speaker with extra credit. One good way to assess the effectiveness of the course could be to record times at the beginning of the course and then record times at the end of the course and see if there's much improvement. Administrators love the concept of making the course accountable. This game could take thirty to forty-five minutes depending on the class size. It could be stretched out to get a "winner" by taking the top students and pitting them against each other.

Question Dialogue Game

This game takes twenty to thirty minutes to complete for a class of twenty-five to thirty students.

Nonsense

This activity takes about twenty minutes for twenty-five to thirty students to complete.

Chapter Two: Self-Introduction Speeches

My classes used the 3-D Collage the first semester and the Interview Activity the second semester because some students often take two of my classes in one year.

3-D Collage

I usually have five students present each day. I use the cards to establish who goes on what day. It takes about fifteen minutes in five to six class sessions to complete a class of twenty-five to thirty.

Self-Presentation Introductory Speech

I usually intersperse speeches during the congress session, because students tend to get restless after a prolonged period sitting and listening to speech after speech. Therefore, I have the class start with five 3-D Collages or six Interviews each day until all the students are done. It takes about twelve to fifteen minutes for five students to present 3-D Collages or six students to complete Interviews. Or, at least two class periods for everyone to present. The card method of random selection governs speaking order.

Chapter Three: Demonstration Speeches

The following activity is a great way to show students the importance of word choice and word selection.

The first day bring a jar of peanut butter, bread, a knife, a plate, and a napkin. Ask the students to tell you how to make a peanut butter sandwich. Take every one of their suggestions literally. For example, if they tell you to put the peanut butter on the bread, take the jar and put it on the bread. Then they may say open the jar first. Then open the jar as if you were going to smash it. They will tell you to unscrew the lid. Then put the peanut butter on the bread. Once the class sees that the peanut butter won't come out of the jar on its own, they will tell you to use the knife. When you start with the handle down going into the peanut butter, they will tell you to use the bladed edge of the knife. Finally, you will get the peanut butter on the bread. This becomes an exercise in clarity and precision in communication. The class has a good time with this activity. After careful instruction, there will be a peanut butter sandwich. This takes about ten to fifteen minutes.

The Project

Students develop unique topics avoiding duplication. Write their topics in the grade book or on the seating chart. My students need two library sessions to research and plan their speeches. Again, use the card system to randomly select speaking order. Plan no more than seven or eight speeches per fifty-minute period. If there is time left over, play one of the games mentioned in Chapter One: The First Day and Breaking the Ice. Also, if students plan to bake cookies or bring food, make sure they go at the beginning of the period. Be sure to remind them to bring adequate napkins, plates, cups, etc. Of course, students aren't expected to feed the class, but some may bring enough of their project to share with everyone.

Give the students the explanation and rubric. Now that they know everyone, they should have a degree of comfort and be ready to speak with more elegance.

You may choose to have the students turn in the Student Comment Sheet (page 123) for a grade. You can then make a summary of all pertinent criticisms to give the speakers.

Chapter Four: Evening News, Sports Broadcasting, and Commercials

Evening News

It takes about two full fifty-five-minute class periods to prepare and an additional one to two class periods to present.

Commercials

The class gets one fifty-five-minute class period to prepare and one class period to perform the skit. Each student needs to bring a prop.

Section Two: The Basics
Chapter Six: Listening

Class Activity 6

I usually have everyone ask a question of at least five students for full credit.

Chapter Nine: Group Dynamics

Despite the accolades, group work in the classroom has one drawback: Rarely do all members of a group contribute equally to a given project. The benefits outweigh this one disadvantage when considering that group decisions and strategies are generally better than individual decisions. If you create the groups based on some writing or speaking sample, then the consistency and the expectation of the group is more or less known. One strategy is for you to assign individual grades and tasks within a group to assess the students.

It is important for the instructor to keep students individually on task and responsible to their groups. One way to achieve this end is to provide students with worksheets that help them track their own individual progress throughout a given assignment. Of course, the individual worksheet displays the necessary steps that the student has taken to accomplish the group goal. The actual group performance shows how all of the students work together to achieve an end.

Chapter Eleven: Cutting Drama and Humor

Sometimes a student's piece does not match the student's skills. The coach then must look to other pieces to make a better fit. Sometimes, a freshman has difficulty competing against juniors and seniors. With maturation and practice, the student improves. Of course, there are pieces that transcend all of the usual barriers. Sometimes a judge's preference will be influenced by the frequency that he or she has seen a given piece. Fresh pieces tend to get the best results.

Chapter Twelve: Basic Debate

The Class Debate

The first type of class debate has the whole class taking sides. One way to control the activity is to regulate who speaks when. You can keep precedence by marking in your grade book or a seating chart who has spoken when. Sometimes this type of debate can get off topic, then you, as moderator, can bring the focus back to the point being discussed. This type of debate can take fifty-five minutes or more of a class period for a group of thirty students. What I do is require each student to participate to earn credit for that day. I offer extra credit for students who positively continue to participate beyond their initial contribution.

The Three-Group Debate

The three-group form of debate may seem unequal because there is a group in the middle who does not need to contribute or be a part of the debate other than moving from undecided to one side or the other — some of them may opt to stay in the middle. What I do is have them take some notes on the salient arguments being presented. They can present their notes to the class and earn a participation grade.

Debate Over the Issues

I usually spend two class periods to have the students research their topics and develop speeches. Make sure they know to research both sides of an issue so they can anticipate the opposing team's arguments.

Moderate the debate as needed. Have a watch handy to keep track of times. Maybe use time signals so the students have an idea how much time they have.

Use one, fifty-five-minute class period for setting up the topics, dividing the class into groups, and dividing the groups into subgroups.

Use one class period to complete two debates with two-person teams. After each debate, I usually point out the positives made by both sides and I include suggestions as to how to argue certain points. The goal here is that the quality of the debates should improve with each subsequent debate.

151

The instructor could make this event last longer by placing teams in competitive brackets and establishing a class champion. I don't recommend this for most classes as many students will feel left out of the activity.

Chapter Thirteen: Student Congress

Controversial Newspaper Article Exercise

It can take up to an hour to present all the articles. If there is time left over, it is fun to play a game to take up the slack.

The next day's homework is to take five articles from different sections of the newspaper, one article per section, and explain in a paragraph why each article is controversial. Be sure to explain the different sections of the newspaper. I usually bring one in and show the students the various sections. They simply hand this in for a grade. This assignment gives the students an understanding as to what is going on in the world and prepares them for the resolution topics they may write.

What Needs to be Changed in Society?

Make sure to note in the grade book or on a seating chart what topics the students choose. They should all have different topics. This activity takes about fifty minutes for the teacher to model and introduce ideas to a class of twenty-five to thirty students.

I allow one fifty-five-minute class period for students to research speeches on others' legislation. They must speak on their own and do a proponent or opponent speech on someone else's legislation.

In this basic public speaking course, it is important to not overburden students with the rules and regulations of a formal congress setting. This chapter serves to get students speaking several times in front of their peers. Most congresses have a maximum requirement of two minutes, but I allow students extra time if their speeches are well prepared.

The Timing of this Section of Congress

It takes about fifteen to twenty minutes to explain how the congress runs and what the individuals say. I ask for a volunteer to be presiding officer and another volunteer to be a clerk or secretary.

It takes an additional twenty-five to thirty minutes of a class period to introduce and vote on a resolution.

A good congress is a fifty-five-minute session and includes ten to twelve speeches and questions. I limit the questions to three per speaker because if a questioner has a point to make, he or she can just give a speech.

I require students to submit a resolution, do an authorship speech, and do at least two proponent or opponent speeches. This unit takes several class periods to complete. Once the docket is done and all resolutions have been debated, the congress session is over.

I allow two fifty-five-minute class periods for students to research information and write their resolutions. Once resolutions are completed, the instructor gathers them and makes a *docket,* a collection of all the legislation in a packet. Each resolution can be labeled A, B, C, and so on. Students should select resolutions from the docket and research them. You can have them do this in class or as homework.You then make copies of the docket and distribute the docket to the students.

Attention-Getting Device: Creating Congress Speeches

After explaining the various options for an AGD, a good activity for the students is to think of a possible attention-getter for their own topic. After several minutes, they present their ideas. The class can have fun with this assignment by selecting the best opener. That person could receive some extra credit or some other form of special recognition.

For a class of twenty-five to thirty students, this attention-getter activity takes about forty-five minutes.

Section Three:
The Competitive Public Speaking Events
Chapter Fifteen: Original Oratory

Expect to spend an hour explaining how to compete in this event, students need constant work on preparation to be competitive.

When dealing with finding topics, you could use the reflection of the students to open a topic for general discussion, or you could ask students what ideas are compelling or intriguing to them.

Chapter Sixteen: Extemporaneous Speaking

Exercises and Activities for Extemporaneous Speaking

Extemporaneous Speaking activities start with access to evidence. You should develop a range of sources for students to research. Students should read the periodicals that you have assembled and cut the articles in full out of them. They place the articles in files that correspond. For example, an evidence box should have files separated in current events like healthcare, Patriot Act, torture, social security, education, teenage obesity, teen violence, etc.

Chapter Seventeen: Cross-Examination

It usually takes me about twenty hours to teach the basics of Cross-Examination.

Exercises and Activities for Cross-Examination Debate

If there is only one team at your school, you can have the students scrimmage each other. Or, you can call a coach and set up a scrimmage with another school. Afterward, you assist the team by going through arguments point-by-point.

Chapter Eighteen: Lincoln-Douglas Debate

This event takes about five hours to teach to a student. A good way to prepare students for this event is to get those with a similar interest to help each other. Another effective teaching method to instruct these events is to have special workshops with those interested in learning about the debate. The National Forensic League in Ripon, Wisconsin, sells final round videos. The NFL also sells instructional videos for coaches seeking to diversify their instruction.

Exercises and Activities for the Lincoln-Douglas Debate

A project you can do with the class after they do their two-page biography of a philosopher is to have the students create their own philosophical textbook, and then the class will have a functional understanding of the ideas possible in a debate.

Section Four: Honing Your Skills with Assignments and Activities

Chapter Nineteen: Readers Theatre

Give the students class time to come up with a good way to interpret scenes. It takes two fifty-five-minute class periods for the students to be adequately prepared and one to two class periods for the students to present their scenes. Provide students defined scenes where they can readily get material from texts. For example, any scene where action takes place could work. If the entire class is reading *The Adventures of Huckleberry Finn,* the students can look to the scenes where things happen. A scene that works well here is where Huck takes part in Tom Sawyer's gang. Another great scene is where Huck dresses up like a girl to avoid being detected and tries to fool a woman.

Chapter Twenty: Choral Reading

I begin this exercise by performing the Lewis Carroll masterpiece, "The Jabberwocky." I use a variety of different voices to illustrate the range of characters open to students.

I limit groups to six members. Students can gather their own materials. Students have written their own songs and brought in lyrics from artists they know. As with Readers Theatre, the assignment takes two fifty-five-minute class periods to prepare and one to two class periods to present.

Chapter Twenty-One: Negotiations

Negotiation Game

Teams will not be looking to gain a point advantage over the other team even though the rules clearly state that the object of the game is for each team to get as many points as possible, regardless of what the other team does. The key for each team to understand is that the number of points earned is based on what the other team selects. They should understand this without any prompting. If both sides select three every time, then each team gets the maximum of points. The selection of three is the obvious choice for those who read the instructions carefully.

What sometimes happens is one group will start by selecting three each time and during the last couple of rounds, that group will con the other group by having them select three and select two or one to gain the advantage. That team destroys their best chance to succeed. What that group has effectively done is sabotage their chances for the maximum points. This game is powerful in teaching the importance of cooperation. This activity can take a full class period to complete.

Once the game is complete, read the following: "Decide whether you have done well. If you did not choose three each time, you lost out on the maximum possible points. Think if the points represented something meaningful. What if each point represented a thousand dollars? Or, what if each point had an impact on a grade?"

Negotiation Activity

The initial offer is for the union to accept or reject. They should caucus and discuss the company's offer and come to an agreement on a counter proposal. I usually give them about ten minutes to look at the proposal and come up with something. While they are discussing the proposal, the company side works on anticipating the union's walk away point.

Chapter Twenty-Three:
The Body Sculpture Activity

Variation One

This variation could take two full class periods to create and share each sculpture.

Variation Two

The instructor could vary the number of participants in each group as desired. This variation would take a full class of twenty-five students about forty-five minutes for all present and share.

Variation Three

The body sculpture activity is a great release after the students have produced an essay or finished with a hard unit. I have used it as part of a final where instead of having an in-class essay, the class works on the body sculpture project. As for variations one and three, I allow classes to select scenes they intend to use and it is on a first-come, first-serve basis.

Chapter Twenty-Four: The Found Poem and Found Story Assignments

The Found Poem

The assignment usually takes about ten to fifteen minutes to present and thirty to forty minutes for the students to produce in class.

The Found Story

The Found Story Assignment takes about fifteen minutes to explain and may take the students several hours to complete properly.

Chapter Twenty-Five: The Vocabulary Skit

Adherence to the provided vocabulary list is hardly a requisite to conduct the vocabulary quiz skit. You can tailor words to match those found in current texts or recent words used on the SAT or ACT exams.

The carrot with this type of test is that students really enjoy giving and taking the quiz in this manner. Also, I provide an added incentive for students to use a literary term in their skit for five extra credit points. They need to explain how they know they used the term at the bottom of the typed skit. To prevent serious grade inflation, I limit their use of literary terms to one extra-credit-worthy term per skit. The test takers can use any term they hear in a skit, identify it, and receive up to one extra credit point per test.

With regard to grouping students to present the tests, my goal is to integrate all types of learners into groups of four to six students for the vocabulary work. The first day of class I have students write a creative or argumentative paper on a prompt I give them. I basically separate them into two groups. Those who seem to be very engaged based on the sophistication of their arguments or the originality of their creativity are marked and separated into different groups. The diagnostic is not perfect, but with the help of previous performance records, I can get a good idea how to develop groups of mixed ability levels. I also try and mix the genders so that there are at least two girls and two boys to a group. Depending on enrollment, this strategy may not work, so instead of leaving a single girl or boy in a group, I usually create all-girl or all-boy groups.

Chapter Twenty-Six: The Storyboard – Make the Drama

Group Storyboard

The first presented option with the storyboard idea requires much interdisciplinary coordination. The beauty of this project is that it is organized along both a horizontal level and a vertical chronological level. It is horizontal in that several skills are required for each group to complete the project. Conversely, the endeavor is vertical in that each group has only a couple of the same chapters to work with.

To begin, the assignment needs to be thoroughly explained. Once students understand the project, they need to figure out who does what. Usually in a group of five or six, there are a couple of students who are more inclined to drawing, painting, etc. Others are more interested in doing something familiar like writing an essay. Yet another group may be interested in writing the script. Another form of vertical integration is where the students are doing the art work with the scriptwriters. In the same group, the two segments of scriptwriters and artists work together so that the script matches the pictures.

The other horizontal component of the assignment emerges when artists and scriptwriters from each group meet with their art and script counterparts from neighboring groups to make sure there is no redundancy. Ultimately, their interaction could form a seamless transition from one part of the story to the next.

Another benefit to this activity is that there are three separate assignments within each group. Students have a limited choice on what they want to do. In the end it is easy for the instructor to grade them individually. Therefore, each member is graded on his or her specific product.

Individual Storyboard

To begin this activity, you should have a television or some screen in the front and center. Then discuss with the class the different media – print versus film. What are the advantages to reading as opposed to watching? What is gained and lost with each mode of delivery?

Post discussion, show the class a scene. A good scene is from *Zoolander* where the characters have a "walk off." Have the students count the number of shots used to complete the scene. Make sure they understand what a shot is. Ask them, "How does getting accustomed to a rapid sequence of shots affect our ability to function in the classroom?"

Point out the camera movements within a single shot. Consider other elements of the setting like lighting and music, if applicable. Also look at the relationship between the camera and the subject. Ask the class, "How might the subtlest change influence the meaning of the frame?" This is where the class can discuss the importance of manipulation, angle, depth, color, shot selection, and symbolism in the background.

When the students are ready to begin the assignment – that is after they have completed the two storyboards and the one six-picture storyboard — tell them to select an important scene from the targeted reading. Make sure they understand that the first frame should establish the setting. Encourage symbolism.

Upon completion of the text storyboard, have students write their rationale as a thematic essay. Essential components could be evidenced by depth of analysis and syntax. Another important element to look for in the storyboard is the accidental or alternative significance unique to the interpretation. The response section could be used as the basis for a good class discussion. Finally, if the students have the materials, they can make a film from the storyboard.

Chapter Twenty-Seven: The Group Story

Ideally, you make groups of five. If the class doesn't fit perfectly into fives, you can adjust the assignment and move along. If a group has only four contributors, then each person inputs an extra segment to the stories.

Once the students have completed their stories, you can have them read and maybe act their favorite story from their group for the class. This all takes a full class period and works on several creative writing skills.

Chapter Twenty-Eight: Class Discussion

Who Has the Answer

There are many ways to present and deliver a class discussion. The *who has the answer* format is an easy way to assess student work over a given homework assignment. I will usually have prepared several questions over a specific topic. I start by having the students go over a chronology of the assignment. It could be a chapter from a text or novel. Then I solicit questions for understanding — what didn't they get? Usually, I mark on their seating chart each of their contributions. Sometimes, if they include a quotation from the text, I will give them two participation points instead of one. If available, I will mark the participation on the seating chart on an overhead so students can see their participation scores instantly. I have to credit Elizabeth Draper, a great colleague and friend for many years, for this system of crediting students. Typically, I will count participation scores upon completion of a novel or topic and then start all over with a blank seating chart.

One aspect of the *who has the answer* discussion format that can be problematic is that often teachers do not allow time for students to respond. As we are in front of class, the time is magnified and often we do not give enough time for adequate response. It is important to allow students to digest the questions and then respond. The time between asking the question and getting the response is crucial to the success of the discussion. One way to see if you as a teacher are allowing enough time is to ask a question and count to yourself and see how far you get before you're compelled to do something else with that question.

Circle-in-a-Circle

The *circle-in-a-circle* discussion is an excellent way to get students to be the center of the classroom. They participate using the prompts you develop. One variation could be for you to organize students to bring their own prompts. If they fail to do so, they cannot participate. This activity can take thirty to forty-five minutes for a class of thirty to complete. As far as grading this activity, students earn a participation grade. If they continue to participate, they earn extra credit.

If room does not permit, another way to set this up is to have the desks arranged in a V-shape with the point of the V facing toward the discussion prompts.

Bring a Friend

The *bring a friend* discussion format is easy to teach and students conduct the class themselves like the *circle-in-a-circle* format. As the teacher, you score the students on their ability to come up with prompts and responses. A good way to prepare the class for this exercise is to return study guides over a chapter or section to students so that their prompts can come directly from those guides, or to tell them to bring a discussion prompt to class as part of a homework assignment. This activity can take a class of thirty students fifty to sixty minutes.

Focus Group

The *focus group* class discussion is another excellent idea from my colleague Katy Miller. The teacher takes the homework assignment and pulls several salient quotations from it. Then, attach questions to each quotation and the student answers a question through a quotation that he or she has found in the text. Students learn to connect their answers using the quotations as evidence. This activity takes about fifteen minutes for students to formulate answers and fifty to sixty minutes to share their answers with the group. The teacher can have other students take notes over the presentations. The teacher can collect those notes for a grade or create a test over the material presented. Students can respond to answers presented and receive credit for their contributions.

Another variation to this format is where students can work in groups to find an answer to a question. This method works well with texts that have several questions after a particular selection or section. One person presents, one person writes, and the others contribute. To make sure that each person in the group does his or her fair share, note who records and who presents. Make sure they rotate duties so everyone has a chance to write and present.

A Fifth Option

Other ways to assess student work in a class discussion includes the reading "merry-go-round." I used to call this the "Gatling gun graded discussion," but changed the name so as to keep politically correct. I ask students randomly, usually via cards with their names on them, what about last night's reading they remember. The only rules: closed book, no talking, no repetition. I am only looking for limited responses so as to leave material for the others. I can assess and record a class of thirty in about two to three minutes.

Chapter Twenty-Nine: Protest Poetry

I start this unit by showing the class some poetry by the Beat poets Kerouac, Ferlinghetti, and Ginsberg, and we go over how we know this poetry is generated by a form of protest. I will show the students a stanza and ask them, "What institution is this poem protesting?" I then cover the protests of the sixties accompanied by the music of protest. We look not only at the music, but the mood of the music. For example, "Where Have All the Flowers Gone" conveys a mood of sadness, whereas "Day of Destruction" illustrates anger. We discuss the origin of protest with the realization that it has been around for thousands of years.

Bibliography

Addington, G.K. (Fall 1995) Personal Communication.

Allen, Mike and Raymond Preiss. "Examining Textbooks: An Analysis Examining Changes over Time." St. Louis, MO: Communication Education Interest Group Central States Communication Association Convention, 1997.

Balcer, Charles L. and Hugh F. Seabury. *Teaching Speech in Today's Secondary Schools*. New York: Holt, Rhinehart, and Winston, 1965.

Beebe, Steven A. and Susan J. Beebe. *Public Speaking: An Audience-Centered Approach*. 7th ed. Englewood Cliffs, NJ: Prentice Hall Inc., 1995.

Bennett, William. "The Hows and Whys of Extemporaneous Commentary." *Rostrum*. March 1990: 24.

Bormann, Ernest G. and N.C. Bormann. *Speech Communication: A Comprehensive Approach*. New York: Harper & Row, Publishers, 1977.

Brooks, William D. and Gustav W. Friederich. *Teaching Speech Communication in the Secondary School*. Boston, MA: Houghton Mifflin Harcourt, 1973.

Buell, Barbara. "Negotiation Strategy: Six Common Pitfalls to Avoid." (http://www.gsb.stanford.edu/news/research/hr_negotiation_strategy.shtml). 2007.

De Stefano, J. (Fall 2009) Personal Communications. "Does Your Youth Program Work?" U.S. Department of Justice, Office of Juvenile Justice and Delinquency Prevention. (http://www.ncjrs.gov/pdffiles1 /ojjdp/179001.pdf). 2000.

Draper, E. (Fall 1999) Personal Communications.

Dunbar, Norah E., Catherine F. Brooks, and Tara Kubicka-Miller. "Oral Communication Skills in Higher Education: Using a Performance-Based Evaluation Rubric to Assess Communication Skills." *Innovative Higher Education*. Volume 31, No. 2, 2006: 118-126.

Elson, E.F. and Alberta Peck. *The Art of Speaking*. 3rd ed. Boston, MA: Ginn and Company, 1970: 153, 338.

Emanuel, Richard. "The Case for Fundamentals of Oral Communication." *Community College Journal of Research and Practice*. Volume 29, No. 2, 2005: 153-162.

Evans, A.L., et al. "Public Speaking in a Democracy." *Journal of Instructional Psychology*. Volume 31, No. 4, 2005: 325-329.

Franklin, Sharon and Deborah J. Clark. *Essentials of Speech Communication*. Evanston: McDougal Littell, 2001.

Grasty, William K. and Mary T. Newman. *Introduction to Basic Speech*. Beverly Hills: Glencoe Press, 1969.

Gray, Giles Wilkeson and Waldo W. Braden. *Public Speaking: Principles and Practice*. New York: Harper, 1951.

Gullicks, Kriste A., Judy C. Pearson, Jeffery T. Child, and Colleen R. Schwab. "Diversity and Power in Public Speaking." *Communication Quarterly.* Volume 53, Issue 2, 2005: 249.

Hayworth, Donald. *An Introduction to Public Speaking.* New York: The Ronald Press Company, 1941.

Hensley, Dana and Diana Carlin. *Mastering Competitive Debate.* 7th ed. Logan, IA: Perfection Learning Corporation, 2005.

Howes, Raymond F. *Historical Studies of Rhetoric and Rhetoricians.* Ithaca, NY: Cornell University Press, 1961.

Hulbert, Jack E. *Effective Communication for Today.* Cincinnati, OH: Thomson South-Western, 1991.

Hunter, Darryl, Trevor Gambell, and Bikkar Randhawa. "Gender Gaps in Group Listening and Speaking: Issues in Social Constructivist Approaches to Teaching and Learning." *Educational Review.* Volume 57, Issue 3, August 2005: 331.

Kelly, Lynne, Gerald M. Phillips, and James A. Kenten. *Teaching People to Speak Well: Training and Remediation of Communication Reticence.* Cresskill, NJ: Hampton Press, 2005.

Lettes, C. (Fall 1999) Personal Communications.

Lewis, George L., Russell I. Everett, James W. Gibson, and Kathryn T. Schoen. *Teaching Speech.* Columbus, OH: Bell and Howell, 1969.

Lionetti, Timothy and Christine Cole. "A Comparison of the Effects of Two Rates of Listening While Reading on Oral Reading Fluency and Reading Comprehension." *Education and Treatment of Children.* Volume 27, No. 2, May 2004: 114-129.

McCall, Roy Clyde. *Fundamentals of Speech: A text-handbook of principles and methods.* New York: The Macmillan Company, 1949.

McCutcheon, Randall, James Schaffer, and Joseph R. Wycoff. *Communication Matters.* Minneapolis/St. Paul, MN: West Publishing Co., 1994.

Magin, Douglas and Phil Helmore. "Peer and Teacher Assessments of Oral Presentation Skills: How reliable are they?" *Studies in Higher Education.* Volume 26, Issue 3, October 2001: 292.

Martin, Howard and William Colburn. *Communication and Consensus: An Introduction to Rhetorical Discourse.* New York, NY: Harcourt, Brace, and Jovanovich, 1972.

Miller, K. (Winter 2010) Personal Communications.

Morreale, Sherwyn P., Michael M. Osborn, and Judy C. Pearson. "Why Communication Is Important: A Rationale for the Centrality of a Discipline." *Journal of the Association of Communication Administration 29.* January, 2000: 1-25.

Nagel, Michael C. "Lend Them an Ear: The Significance of Listening to Children's Experiences of Environmental Education." *International Research in Geographical and Environmental Education.* Volume 13, No. 2, 2004: 115.

Nelson, Marilyn. "The Fruit of Silence." *Teachers College Record*. Volume 108, No. 9, September 2006: 1733-1741.

Oberg, Brent C. *Forensics: The Winner's Guide to Speech Contests*. Colorado Springs, CO: Meriwether Publishing Ltd., 1995.

Oberg, Brent C. *Speechcraft*. Colorado Springs, CO: Meriwether Publishing Ltd., 1994.

Ogilvie, Mardel. *Teaching Speech in the High School*. New York: Appleton-Century-Crofts Inc., 1961.

Persi, Nina C. and William N. Denman. "Civic Responsibility as a Justification for the Teaching of Public Speaking: An Analysis of Basic Course Textbooks." Huntington, WV: Marshall University, 1997.

Public Law 95-561, amending Title II of the Elementary and Secondary Education Act of 1965.

Reid, Loren. *Teaching Speech Fourth Edition*. New York: McGraw-Hill, 1971.

Reppert, James E. "Improving Communication Textbooks through Rigorous Processes of Revision and Review." Gilbersville, KY: paper presented at the Kentucky Communication Association and the Tennessee Communication Association Convention, September 2001: 14-15.

Robinson, Karl F. and Kerikas, E. J. *Teaching Speech: Methods and Materials*. NY: David McKay Company Inc., 1963.

Rodenburg, Patsy. *The Right to Speak: Working with the Voice*. New York: Routledge Inc., 1992.

Saffire, William. *Lend Me Your Ears: Great Speeches in Human History*. New York: W.W. Norton & Company, 1992.

Sanford, William P. and Willard Hayes Yeager. *Principles of Effective Speaking*. New York: Thomas Nelson and Sons, 1930.

Sanford, William P. and Willard Hayes Yeager. *Principles of Effective Speaking*. New York: The Ronald Press Company, 1942.

Sauls, K. (Fall 1999) Personal Communication.

Scheidel, Thomas M. *Speech Communication and Human Interaction*. Glenview, IL: Scott, Foresman and Co, 1972.

Sprague, Jo. "Communication Education: The Spiral Continues." *Communication Education*. Volume 51, No. 4, October 2002: 337-354.

Stadler, Marie A. and Gay Cuming Ward. "Supporting the Narrative Development of Young Children." *Early Childhood Education Journal*. Volume 33, No. 2, October 2005: 73.

Student Congress Manual. 2001 Edition. Ripon, WI: National Forensic League, 2001.

Tanner, Fran Averett. *Creative Communication: Projects in Acting, Speaking, Oral Reading*. 5th ed. Topeka, KS: Clark Publishing Inc., 1996.

Thompson, Kathy, Pamela Leintz, Barbara Nevers, and Susan Witkowski. "The Integrative Listening Model: An Approach to Teaching and Learning Listening." *The Journal of General Education*. Volume 53, No. 3-4, 2004: 225-226.

Verderber, Rudolph F. *Speech for Effective Communication.* 2nd ed. Austin, TX: Holt Rinehart and Winston, 1994.

Weaver, Andrew Thomas. *Speech: Forms and Principles.* New York: Longmans, Green, 1951.

White, Eugene Edmond. *Practical Speech Fundamentals.* New York: The MacMillan Company, 1960.

Winebrenner, Susan. *Teaching Kids with Learning Difficulties in the Regular Classroom.* Minneapolis, MN: Free Spirit Publishing, 1996.

Witt, Paul L. and Ralph R. Behnke. "Anticipatory Speech Anxiety as a Function of Public Speaking Assignment Type." *Communication Education.* Volume 55, No. 2, April 2006: 167-177.

Worley, David W., Debra A. Worley, and David McMahan. "A Descriptive Analysis of Best-Selling Basic Course Texts." Terre Haute, IN: Indiana State University, 1999.

Yip, Elijah. *The Enlightened Storyteller.* Taos, NM: CDE Publications, 1995.

Permissions Acknowledgements

William H. Bennett: Excerpt from *Rostrum* magazine, copyright © 2010 William H. Bennett/CDE.

Fran Tanner: Excerpt from *Creative Communication: Projects in Acting, Speaking, Oral Reading* (5th Ed). © 1996. Used with permission of Perfection Learning Corporation.

About the Author

Michael Gallagher was born in Denver, Colorado. He went to school at the University of Colorado and began his teaching career while working for Proctor and Gamble in Japan. But it was in high school where he learned about the world of speech and debate. He worked as a speech and debate coach for twenty years. Then, with the support of an open-minded school administration, he was selected to participate in the Fulbright program. He worked in Istanbul, Turkey, during the 2005-2006 school year. Currently, he teaches language arts at Heritage High School in Littleton, Colorado, where he has taught for the last twelve years. He lives with his wife and son in nearby Englewood. He loves his wife, students, and colleagues, and it is only through their gracious understanding has he had the freedom to complete this book.